KERRY PACKER

Tall tales & true stories

KERRY PACKER
Tall tales & true stories

Michael Stahl

hardie grant books
MELBOURNE · LONDON

Published in 2015 by Hardie Grant Books

Hardie Grant Books (Australia)
Ground Floor, Building 1
658 Church Street
Richmond, Victoria 3121
www.hardiegrant.com.au

Hardie Grant Books (UK)
5th & 6th Floor
52–54 Southwark Street
London SE1 1RU
www.hardiegrant.co.uk

A Cataloguing-in-Publication entry is available from the catalogue of the National
Library of Australia at www.nla.gov.au
Packer: Tall tales and true stories
ISBN 9781742708508

Publisher: Pam Brewster
Cover design: Design by Committee
Typeset in 11.5/15t pt Stempel Garamond Roman by Kirby Jones
Printed in Australia by Griffin Press

The paper this book is printed on is certified against the Forest
Stewardship Council® Standards. Griffin Press holds FSC chain of
custody certification SGS-COC-005088. FSC promotes environmentally
responsible, socially beneficial and economically viable management of
the world's forests.

FSC
www.fsc.org
MIX
Paper from
responsible sources
FSC® C009448

For the quiet achievers.

CONTENTS

'The ultimate purgatory would be to go to the Opera House and hear Joan Sutherland sing.'

KERRY PACKER, IN 1977

INTRODUCTION

It is possible that no individual has been more influential in shaping Australia's culture than Kerry Francis Bullmore Packer, AC. For 30 years, via his Consolidated Press Holdings, Kerry Packer controlled television's perennial ratings leader Channel Nine and as much as 60 per cent of the nation's magazine market.

The majority of what Australians actually watched, read and believed in the latter part of the 20th century came through the prism of Packer.

The average Australian might reasonably question the qualifications of a jet-owning, polo-playing, globe-trotting billionaire to determine the relevance of *Seinfeld* or sewing patterns to their daily lives.

But beneath all the billionaire clutter, Kerry Packer had quite a bit in common with large sections of Australian society: a cheeky humour, a competitive drive, love for his kids, a passion for sports and movies. No-one would more begrudgingly don a dinner suit than the billionaire eating burgers in front of the television.

Packer was a paradox: known to all, known by few.

Born into great wealth, the younger of two sons had a childhood punctuated by a life-threatening case of polio, stints in boarding schools and apparently little attention from his strict and detached parents. He was sent to some of Australia's most exclusive and academically admired schools, but was notable mainly for his efforts in sports. This included boxing, both sanctioned and spontaneous.

The baron of publishing was dyslexic. He bulldozed right through it: 'I don't read much, but I spend a lot of time talking to people who do.' The son dismissed by his father as 'boofhead' inherited a business in 1974 valued at perhaps $100 million. When he died 31 years later on Boxing Day 2005, he handed his own son James control of a media, property, agriculture and gambling empire worth $6.9 billion.

Kerry Packer made the bulk of his fortune from the media, but he vigorously shunned its intrusion into his own or his family's life. Adventurous journalists were very quickly met with legal and even physical threats. He gave interviews sparingly and only, it seemed, when it suited a particular political or business ambition.

Privately, Packer was known to enjoy one-on-one lunches and telephone conversations with trusted friends and staff that would last for hours. He would natter about weather, sports, anything. 'He would sit with smart people and just suck their brains out', is how one former executive put it.

Those who knew him understood Packer's empathy for the man in the street. In the days after Packer's passing, Garry Linnell, the then editor in chief of the flagship *The Bulletin*, remembered this advice from his boss:

'Out there, there are many of them earning—what's the average wage? About 50K? They're earning that, and some a lot less. How do they get by on that? How do you raise a family and pay a mortgage and just do what you have to do? Don't forget 'em. You journos always do.'

This book seeks not to glorify Kerry Packer, but to expose more of his humour and humanity; qualities that were strategically kept close.

'Arrived Melbourne safely. No love, Kerry.'

According to Kerry, this was the telegram he sent to his parents, after they made him get back on a train from Sydney to Geelong to retrieve a tennis racquet

I'm grateful to say I never formally met Kerry Packer. To a mere deputy editor on two of his successful motoring magazines between 1983–90, a summoning to the chairman's office on the third floor would have been highly unusual and possibly terminal.

Among the young employees of my ilk, Mr Packer was a mysterious force that pervaded the building. Actual sightings were rare. Yet our cheeky nickname 'Uncle Kerry' (whispered, after a shoulder-check) conveyed the respect and affection felt for the proprietor who empowered us to produce the best magazines we could. They carried our reputations, as well as his.

Only twice in my six years at Park Street did I see Mr Packer in person. Both occasions were close encounters; both involved elevators.

I was waiting in the foyer to meet a colleague. There was a sudden flurry of activity, with three or four security staff erupting through a side entrance. One mouthed hurriedly into his walkie-talkie: 'Visitor has arrived, visitor has arrived.'

In the next instant, the quite breathtakingly tall figure of the chairman swept through the door, surging past me towards the lifts. The burly security guards looked like tugboats flitting around a nuclear-powered aircraft carrier.

About a year later, I would have a much closer encounter, riding wordlessly in the lift in the exclusive company of Kerry Packer AC. (I'm thankful it wasn't the lift car in which someone had scratched "Packer can't play baccarat" into the stainless steel panel).

Recalling the experience now, I'm in awe of the quick wit and opportunist instinct of one well-known, knockabout writer with *The Picture* magazine, who often told the story of being alone in an elevator with the chairman—when the lift lurched to a halt between floors.

Packer jabbed at the lift buttons. Then grabbed the emergency phone. It's not known who answered, but the lift's other occupant was able to imagine a telephone receiver being held 10 centimetres from a smoking column of cervical vertebrae.

Packer slammed the phone back onto its hook. The elevator became a cosmic sinkhole of silence.

The writer chirped: 'Gee, I hope they fix this soon. I don't know about you, but I've got work to do.'

When it was my turn, I was too dumbstruck by Packer's presence to say anything.

The elevator had arrived at my floor and the doors opened. It had one occupant. My eyes climbed slowly up the man-mountain in front of me. Not only was Kerry Packer 15 centimetres taller than me, and more than half as heavy again; facing him, he seemed to taper upwards to infinity.

In a millisecond, I had to weigh the dilemma of possibly breaching protocol by entering the lift, or being seen to waste time by waiting for the next one. I smiled weakly, stepped aboard, and rode a while in his great shadow.

Kerry Packer was larger than life, but very much *in* life. This book is a collection of stories, gathered from people who knew him, from those who have documented him, and from the folklore that inevitably grew up around him. At heart, they're just stories of a remarkable Australian.

Kerry Packer was probably destined to be remarkable—one way or another. He was born on 17 December 1937 into circumstances that rarely seem to produce inconsequential types. A look through the ledger of Gettys, Hearsts, Fords and Kennedys suggests that a child in this kind of family could turn out as either a brilliant and respectable scion, or a frustrated and rebellious dropout.

In young Kerry's case, for a long time the odds appeared to be stacked towards the latter. And if the popular version of Packer family history is to be believed, the tallest hurdle to acceptance was his tough and uncompromising father, Sir Frank.

In the 1979 book *As The Twig Is Bent*, Kerry said of his father: 'There are any number of people who can go out and

'Frank Packer was described as tough, shrewd, robust, just as game as they come. And I think there's always been this element in the talk about Frank and Kerry Packer, that they're sort of quintessential red-blooded anti-intellectual, anti-authoritarian sports-loving Aussie blokes.'

DR BRIDGET GRIFFEN-FOLEY, BIOGRAPHER OF SIR FRANK PACKER, INTERVIEWED BY ABC RADIO ON THE DAY OF PACKER'S STATE MEMORIAL SERVICE, 17 FEBRUARY 2006

'I see you're a Communist. You're fired.'

Supposedly Sir Frank, to an employee who made the fashion error of wearing a red cardigan to work fly a jumbo jet, but there's a very elite group of people who can design it and make it work, and my father was a designer and a person who could make things work … I was able to fly the plane he built, but I couldn't have built it.'

According to Kerry, Sir Frank's Consolidated Press empire was founded on an inheritance from *his* father, the gruff, tough *Smith's Weekly* newspaper pioneer, R C Packer, who died in 1934. Kerry estimated that inheritance at £10,000, around $175,000 in today's money—though many figured it had been rather more.

In 1931, at just 25 years of age, Frank had already made a small fortune from a masterful piece of publishing bluffery, involving the mooted launch of a cheaper rival to Sydney's *Sun*. The innovative *Australian Women's Weekly*, launched in 1933, gave the Packer play even more momentum.

Tales of Sir Frank Packer were legend around Australian Consolidated Press (as it was known from 1957), even decades after his death in 1974. He was said to have often returned to the office from long, late dinners and randomly fired any employees who happened, through diligence, to be still at their desks.

'Younger journalists would be often distressed by this, and the older hands would say, "Don't worry about it, just come back in on Monday",' says Patrick Cook. The cartoonist worked on several ACP titles, including *The Bulletin* and *Cleo*.

The late Donald Horne, who served many years on Packer's *Daily Telegraph* and *The Bulletin*, recounted in his 1985 memoir *Confessions of a New Boy* being sacked for taking a company car on an assignment to rural Cessnock, 160 kilometres from Sydney. Frank blasted him for not catching a bus.

Another employee, it was said, made the fashion error of wearing a red cardigan to work. On seeing this, Sir Frank observed, 'I see you're a Communist. You're fired.'

A favourite story concerned a young lad who was leaning on a desk, apparently chatting up the receptionist. Sir Frank strode up and collared him from behind. 'What's your pay each week?' he thundered. 'Thirty dollars, sir,' said the startled kid. Sir Frank thrust his hand in his pocket, leafed out a wad of notes and thrust them into the kid's hand. 'There's four weeks' pay. You're fired!'

As the kid slunk off down the hall, the chairman barked after him: 'What department were you from?' To which the kid replied, 'I don't work here. I'm a courier.'

Paul Barry, in *The Rise and Rise of Kerry Packer*, reported a different version, centred on Sir Frank's unwritten claim on a particular lift in the Park Street building. The doomed 'employee' who happened to be inside when it stopped in front of the raging Sir Frank was a deliveryman from the Post Office.

The elevator attitude chimes with Patrick Cook's recollection. 'That's what they said about Frank: "It's Frank's world, you're just living in it."'

Despite the Packer wealth, it cannot have been a cushy childhood for sons Clyde, born on 22 July 1935, and Kerry two years later. Kerry, however, would always staunchly defend his 'strict, but magnificent' father and his mother Gretel who, he said, 'believed that her function in life was to look after her husband and I don't disagree with that.'

When he was five, Kerry was sent to boarding school— in Cranbrook, just a few hundred metres from the family home in Sydney's elite Bellevue Hill. The threat of Japanese invasion prompted his parents to send him to live with an aunt in Bowral, 120 kilometres south-west of Sydney. There, at age seven, he contracted polio, the disease that paralysed lungs and limbs and left many children from the mid-1940s with lifelong, crippling injuries.

Kerry spent nine months in a Sydney hospital in an iron lung, before being dispatched to Canberra under the care of a nurse. He spent two years there, making a total of four years away from his parents.

As told in *As The Twig Is Bent*: 'I had seen nothing of them, except for seeing my mother perhaps half a dozen times. It was the war and my father was working for the army and my mother worked hard in the Red Cross. It wasn't a matter of their not wanting to see me, it was a matter of getting on and doing things, which is something that I believe was right.'

Illness, long absences and as yet-undiagnosed dyslexia conspired to make the remainder of Packer's schooling a chore. He directed his energies instead towards sport, and at Geelong Grammar in Victoria, where he was sent to board at age 12 or 13, he was a vigorous competitor in everything from boxing and rugby to cricket and tennis.

The latter sport gave rise to one of Packer's better-known school stories, which he told with some glee in a *Parkinson in Australia* interview in 1979. The young Kerry had returned to Sydney just hours earlier from Geelong, a formidable, day-long journey, and was playing snooker with his father. Kerry's mother, unpacking his bag, called down that she couldn't find his tennis racquet.

'Eventually the old man's done his lolly at this,' Kerry recounted. 'He said, "For Christ's sake Gretel, do you want me to send him back to pick [it] up?" And she's not going to be outdone at this stage. She said, "Yes". And the next thing I know, I'm on a train back to Melbourne.'

Interviewer Michael Parkinson enquired, 'What did you do when you got there?'

'Oh, I just sent him a telegram and said, you know, "Arrived Melbourne safely. No love, Kerry."'

It was never in doubt that the sons would follow Frank into the family business. Kerry was dispatched to work in the machine room where first the *Daily Telegraph*, and later the *Australian Women's Weekly* was printed. It was hard, dirty, physical work that involved cleaning the enormous presses and lugging away bundled newspapers and magazines.

Sir Frank may have designed and built the plane, but he had little faith in his younger son's ability to ever take the controls. Clyde, meanwhile, was already rising through the editorial suites.

Clyde Packer had been an accomplished student at Sydney's Cranbrook school and later, Geelong Grammar. Erudite and articulate, he was the heir-apparent from central casting. Clyde was made a director of Australian Consolidated Press at age 21 and editor-in-chief of the artsy fortnightly *The Observer* magazine at 22.

With his progressive attitudes, however, Clyde would not be a great admirer of his father. The relationship at Channel Nine, which he described as 'a very equitable arrangement: I had the responsibility and he had the authority', eventually reached critical mass. In 1972, Clyde resigned from the family business and effectively, from the family's control.

'He was an intensely agreeable man who, unusually, wore a kaftan at all times,' remembers Patrick Cook, who worked on one of Clyde's first ventures as an independent publisher, the risqué sex advice magazine *Forum*. 'He was the brains that [Sir] Frank wanted to leave everything to.'

Clyde's split from the Packer program left Sir Frank with only one other heir. And, Sir Frank was in poor health, with steadily worsening heart and respiratory conditions.

Kerry Packer assumed the role of chairman on the death of his father on 1 May 1974. For all his defence of his father, some close to him—like advertising man John Singleton and cricket star Tony Greig—knew the truth. Singleton rarely breaks his silence on the subject of his mate 'Kerro', but in the 2006 documentary *Big Fella: The Extraordinary Life of Kerry Packer*, he revealed: 'The happiest moment of his life, by a mile, was the day his dad died. He told me that on half a dozen occasions.'

Clyde would complete his detachment from the family business in 1976, selling his share to his younger brother and departing for a new life in Northern California. In an eerie coincidence, Clyde would receive a kidney transplant at the age of 63, the same age at which Kerry would receive his. Clyde died in the Santa Barbara Cottage Hospital in 2001, aged 65.

Part 1
BUILDING THE EMPIRE

'He would push you, see if there were any cracks in the armour ... That was the way he got ahead. He understood things, and he made sure people knew what they were doing just by constantly questioning. He made sure he got all the answers.'

GRAHAM LAWRENCE, FORMER ACP ADVERTISING EXECUTIVE

1

PARK STREET

It's hard for most Australians to think of Kerry Packer without the familiar suffix: Australia's richest man. Yet those who worked with him in the extraordinary era of the early 1970s—as he began to build the hugely successful stable of magazines that would become an empire—got to see an uncertain, chrysalis-like character emerging from the shell of his father's scorn and criticism.

Cleo magazine had its origins in a derailed deal with Hearst to publish its *Cosmopolitan* title in Australia. *Cosmopolitan* magazine was catching the new wave of feminism sweeping across the world, but the Packers' arch-rival in publishing, John Fairfax Ltd, was first to jump on board.

Ita Buttrose, an ambitious section editor on Packer's *Telegraph*, had already mocked up an alternative. Packer flicked through the mock-up and, as Buttrose related in her autobiography *Early Edition: My First Forty Years*, he smiled at her: 'Right. We'll publish this one. I want it on the streets six months before the Australian edition of *Cosmopolitan* comes out.' And that's how things operated at 54 Park Street, headquarters of Packer's beloved ACP.

Sir Frank Packer, by then no longer a healthy man, flatly opined that the alternative being pushed by his son—its name shortened to *Cleo* from Buttrose's original proposal, *Cleopatra*—was bound to fail. He gave Kerry his approval to go ahead, but the old man's motive was quite possibly to see his second son stumble and be put back in his box.

Andrew Cowell, from *Belle* magazine, was the art director singled out by Buttrose to design the groundbreaking *Cleo*, the first issue of which appeared in November, 1972. Cowell dealt with Packer almost daily, in the unexpected setting of the proprietor wandering up to his desk and stealing Cowell's cigarettes.

Cowell, then in his early 20s, says he found Packer, by then in his mid-30s, always interesting and interested. And not especially intimidating. 'Everyone just saw him as Ita's boss. In those days, you still had Sir Frank, Harry Chester, David McNicoll. Kerry was very much the new generation.'

'He'd always just sit down and start talking about something. He'd ask what I was doing, then go off into a story about something. And he was always giving insights.

'I remember him telling me once that it's really important to understand the business you're involved in. He said that's why he appreciated working on the presses—and he did understand print really, really well. He said he can service a TV camera—but only just, he said, because he'd learned on the ones with valves and now they were coming with transistors.

'He said, "It's really important to know how things work, son, 'coz otherwise they'll con you ..."'

Cowell was seeing the early evidence of Packer's ability to soak in opinion and information, feeding the gut instinct that first found its voice in *Cleo*, and would later make Channel Nine into the powerhouse of television.

'*Cleo* was his,' Cowell says. 'He created it, he gave the people who created it the room to breathe. It was, "If you think it's a good idea, go for it."'

'It was a time when it was all changing really quickly, it was really exciting. Photography was changing dramatically, people were starting to use a lot more colour. Up till then, if you were really lucky, you might have one-third of a magazine in colour; *Cleo* was 50/50.'

'What my father did was to take everything he had, all the prospects of everything he ever had and put it on one roll of the dice. And what happens with great men and creators is that they work so hard with so little. Now I might risk more than the next guy, but I've never risked the lot. I've never risked anything that's going to put Consolidated Press at risk; might knock it around for a year or two, but we don't take the sort of risks where everything depends on it going right.'

Kerry Packer in 1979, *As The Twig Is Bent*

'So ... we go down and see Kerry Packer and I said, there's not enough money in this whole marketplace to make these magazines profitable. And Kerry says: "What if we turn it into a monthly, and you get a million circulation, what sort of ad rates can you get then, and how many pages can you get"—just bang-bang-bang.

And a few months later, it was a monthly. It got to 1.25 million circulation and made money for years and years and years.'

GRAHAM LAWRENCE

'I think he was a fantastic Australian. Just building that publishing company, from just two magazines to the biggest magazine publisher in the country—which employed so many creative people.'

Andrew Cowell, founding art director, *Cleo* magazine

'TREVOR, GET YOUR ARSE HERE.'

'I heard the story—apocryphal, mind—that Kerry was in Las Vegas, rang Trevor Kennedy [then editor of *The Bulletin*] at two o'clock in the morning ... So Trevor had to get on a plane, got himself to Vegas, waited at the hotel for two hours until, eventually, Kerry came out. Kerry said: "That fucking front cover you had on *The Bulletin* is a disgrace. Don't ever do it again." And that was that ... Uhh, you couldn't have said that on the phone? But that wasn't the point.'

ANDREW COWELL, FOUNDING ART DIRECTOR ON *CLEO*, LATER CREATIVE DIRECTOR OF ACP MAGAZINES

'I don't think he swore a lot. But I'd grown up in a sporting environment, so what someone else might think was a lot of swearing, I'd probably have thought was normal punctuation.'

Greg Chappell

Cartoonist Patrick Cook was another early contributor to *Cleo*. He, too, recalls an electric atmosphere where, in the months after *Cleo*'s zeroine-to-heroine ascendancy, anything seemed possible.

'I can't think of anything that was mentioned to me that Kerry had rejected as an idea—the centrefold, the sealed sections. It was very bold for its time. I think he was more prepared to take a chance and see if it sold. And when it sold, that did it.'

Ita Buttrose, speaking to George Negus in 2004 on ABC TV's *George Negus Tonight*, recalled that Kerry Packer wasn't always entirely fearless. 'The only time I ever remember Kerry looking a bit pale was in the very early days of *Cleo*, when we were putting in a story about how female masturbation could help overcome frigidity ...'

Still, Kerry Packer was prepared to try anything that would tickle *Cleo*'s readers, for every circulation gain meant another finger-salute at Sir Frank.

Packer wandered over to Cowell one day for the customary smoke, greeting the art director with: 'Son, you look like shit. You need a break. Why don't you go and have a look at what's happening in other publishing companies around the world? Go to America, go to Europe.'

Cowell says he wasn't quite sure what this meant. But he mentioned it to Buttrose and—in the way that things worked when Kerry Packer wanted something done—a wad of plane tickets and traveller's cheques was soon lobbed wordlessly on Cowell's desk.

Cowell's trip lasted three weeks, most of that time spent in his native London, with a few days' stopover on the way home to visit printers in Hong Kong. Cowell gorged himself on the smorgasbord of European magazines available in London. It was one of these—a German magazine—that gave *Cleo* its titillating sealed section, and Cowell one of his most treasured 'cigarette-break moments'.

On his return Cowell presented the German magazine to the *Cleo* printers, who stood there, shaking their heads. The sealed section, they said, was too complicated to produce.

'That's when Kerry came in, grabbed a cigarette—"And what are you guys talking about?" And these two guys obviously thought, "Oh shit." I said, "Oh, we're just trying to do this, but apparently it's really complex …" I thought they were telling me the truth, to be honest. I was sure the Germans were the only ones who could do it.

'Kerry said: "Bullshit! All you've got to do is move the turning arm so it doesn't fold short, then it will only trim off that length."'

Cowell was gobsmacked by his boss's knowledge of printing and binding, though he shouldn't have been, given Packer's hard, grinding apprenticeship. The two printers, caught bang to rights, snivelled: 'Yes, yes, we'll investigate that method, Mr Packer.'

'Don't investigate it. It will fucking work.'

Cleo was a tearaway success.

Two years later, Cowell had relocated to London, floating around the magazine scene. In early-1979, he got a call from Ita Buttrose, asking if he'd consider returning to Sydney. Two nights later, Packer called two night later and made an offer. Cowell remembers it along the lines of 'get your arse back here'. By the time Cowell reached his London desk the following morning, there sat a manila envelope with the necessary paperwork.

If there's one word that comes up often in discussion about Kerry Packer (aside from the favourite, four-letter one), it's 'loyalty'.

'Oh, loyalty was an enormous thing to him,' says Cowell. 'Huge. I think if he ever thought you were trying to take the piss you were in deep trouble. If, on the other hand you were good and you worked hard, I think it was very much appreciated.'

Back at ACP, Cowell was soon named overall creative director. About a year after his return, he committed to buying a small house in Sydney's inner west.

Cowell approached ACP managing director Rob Henty and asked: 'Mr Henty, I want to buy a house and I need a deposit. Is there any way I could borrow it?'

'I've got to say that Kerry was a great person to work with. You know, he was a lot of fun. He had this fantastic sense of humour. He had this natural curiosity—we thought alike. If I went to see him with a big idea, he could see where I was heading. And you know—vice-versa. We could immediately grasp the big ideas that each of us had. And it's a very rare thing when this happens. And it's really exciting.'

ITA BUTTROSE, *AUSTRALIAN STORY*, ABC TV, 15 AUGUST 2011

'The first time I met the bloke [Packer] I was in a lift coming down from the by then notorious seventh floor, home of *People* and *The Picture*. I was dressed, if that's the word, as Tubs Grogan. In one arm I held a stuffed goat. Over my shoulder was an enormous squid's tentacle and next to me was the model, a diminutive stripper with surgically enhanced breasts, denim shorts ...

'The last thing you wanted to happen when you were in the lift under such circumstances was to have anyone get in from the intervening floors. The women's mags on levels five and six detested us. Even worse was the lift stopping at level three. Mahogany Row. Kerry's Lair.

'That day we got past the sheilas' floors but were stopped at three. Kerry got in. He looked at me. I looked at him. He looked at the girl, then looked at me. "Who are you?" he asked.

"Tubs Grogan, Mr Packer. *Picture* magazine."

'There was a short pause. "Carry on," he said.'

Pat Shiel, while working on ACP's lowbrow, but highly successful *People* magazine in the early 1990s (writing under the pseudonym Tubs Grogan).

'One of the accountant guys used to come in and he'd always open the silver cigarette buckets on the table there [in the Tap Room], and take a smoke out. And finally, Kerry turned around to him one day and said: "There's no fuckin' law about not bringing your *own* cigarettes in here, y'know."'

Graham Lawrence

'... for some of us the early evening was a potentially productive time and so we tried to ration our appearances [in the Tap Room]. KP's personal assistant at that time, Pat Wheatley, would occasionally phone me in a tizz on the infamous internal phone system ... frantically communicating that that night's attendance was disappointing or that KP was looking a bit bored or whatever, and could I drop everything and join them. It was not a request you could refuse without a very decent alibi.'

Richard Walsh, former publisher at ACP

Cowell grins as he recalls: 'Literally two to three hours later Rob Henty said, "Come up and see me." So I went up and there was this little letter that said ACP had loaned Andrew Cowell, interest-free, repayable on demand, the amount of $10,000 ... The next morning I went to the bank and there it was.'

A couple of years passed. Happy as Cowell was at ACP, the opportunity to change tack and edit a magazine at another publishing house was a challenge he couldn't resist. But there remained the matter of the $10,000 loan, which he'd made no effort to pay off.

'So I had to call Rob Henty and say, "Mr Henty, I'm actually resigning and I want to leave quite quickly, because I've been offered this job I really want to do ... My big concern is obviously that I owe you $10,000." He went and had a chat to the boss, and then I get the call: "Mr Packer would like to see you."

'So I went up there and he says, "Son, you've got a real problem. You owe me money." And then he asked why was I going, what was I going to do.

'I think he really enjoyed winding me up. And then he said, "Well, what are we going to do about this, then?", holding up this piece of paper. I said, 'Obviously I can't pay it all back now, but I'm very happy to come to any arrangement with you'. He was being very friendly, except for the slightly menacing bits.

'He just said: "Listen, you've done a fantastic job for us, and I think you've helped make me a shitload of money." And he just tore up the piece of paper. "Let's call it quits. Best of luck. And son, if it doesn't work out, you ring me first."

'And I did go back, but I never really had that much to do with him again. By that time, Kerry was right up in the stratosphere, you never really saw him.'

A decade after the shaky foundations of *Cleo* were laid, Packer's confidence in his stewardship of the magazine empire was total—cemented, in part, by his trust in his loyal and creative staff.

Cleo was the first of many successful magazines ACP launched with Kerry at the helm. Other star titles included

Harper's Bazaar, Ralph, Madison and *NW*. All with high circulation figures and reaping big advertising dollars at their peak.

Not all their ideas hit home, of course. One of those rejected titles sits fondly among Cowell's memories of Kerry Packer.

'Ita and I were doing a dummy for a new men's magazine, before he went and got *Australian Playboy*. The dummy for that was called *Packer's*. The Packer name was very much the quintessential Aussie male, brash arrogant, confident—we thought it was a good name. But he looked at the front cover and went, "Nah."'

Adjacent to Kerry Packer's sprawling Park Street office on level three was The Tap Room, a small lounge area where executives were invited—nay, expected—to attend informal, end-of-week drinks. Receiving that first phone call from Packer's PA was like being a 'made guy' in the Mafia.

Not everyone would feel inclined to loiter of an evening, but the Tap Room sessions were a good forum for keeping communications open around the Consolidated Press group. More importantly, they were about keeping the Boss entertained.

The Tap Room was very much the inner sanctum, where Packer would sometimes tell—and sometimes even tolerate—stories against himself.

'One day in his office, he looked me up and down and said, "Son, were you born a dickhead, or did you become one when I hired you?" That was the opening gambit after 10 minutes of incredible anguish and waiting. He would try this on and you'd sometimes have to call his bluff. And on that day I said, "Oh, I think the verdict's pretty overwhelming that I was born a dickhead, I've had a lot of people tell me long before you raised it." And with that he smiled and said, "Sit down son, would you like a cup of tea?" ... He admired a bit of chutzpah.'

Garry Linnell, former editor of *The Bulletin*

'I just enjoyed the sport of it all. You didn't know if you would be there again the next day, or have your heart ripped out on the spot.'

Former ACP magazine executive

'Normally he kept the roaring-off to his office. You were in there watching the painting behind his desk of a lion disembowelling some unfortunate beast, having [Packer] roaring at you ... You got the feeling that you'd better do better in future.'

TREVOR SYKES, FORMER EDITOR, *THE BULLETIN*

'You'd be summoned to his office and his PA said, "Mr Packer wants to see you." You'd ask, "What's it about?" and sometimes she'd give you a heads-up—"Ooh, he's not too happy"—and you knew you were in for a bit of a slapping ... That's when you have that sphincter-puckering moment, and you'd manage to waddle your way over to his part of the office.

'He summoned me in and made me stand in front of his desk for about five minutes while he pretended to read something. Of course, he was dyslexic, and not one of the great readers of all time, and he'd be sitting pretending to read something and he'd have a cigarette burning and then he'd finally look up at you.

'He wouldn't say anything. He'd just wait and see if your Adam's Apple started bobbing up and down like a department store lift in a Boxing Day sale, and you're swallowing as hard as you can, trying to muster a bit of moisture in your mouth ...'

GARRY LINNELL, EDITOR OF *THE BULLETIN* 2002–06, ON HIS FIRST VISIT TO KERRY PACKER'S OFFICE. THE TWO THEN SAT FOR 90 MINUTES, TALKING ABOUT EVERYTHING FROM GAMBLING TO ANZAC HISTORY.

FACING THE BULL ELEPHANT

Television shows like *Dynasty* and *Dallas* would have us believe that tycoons all inhabit opulent, oak-panelled and art-directed offices worthy of colonial statesmen or homecoming polar expeditions. The image didn't quite carry to Kerry Packer's office on the third floor of Australian Consolidated Press headquarters in Park Street, Sydney.

KP's office is most frequently described with its dominant paintings of a lion astride a fresh kill, and a bull elephant, its back to the rest of the herd, staring straight over Packer's head at the occupants of the 1970s-style, plush teal visitor's chairs. Directly opposite his chair was a large television monitor which was almost always on.

Leading up to the office, and its adjoining Tap Room bar area, the walls of 'Mahogany Row' were lined with almost 50 original Norman Lindsay cartoons and drawings from the then century-old archives of *The Bulletin*. But Packer's office reflected his tastes as a Fanta-from-the-can and B&H man.

'By the standards of the rising corporate brilliance of the day, it was rather a modest office,' recalls Trevor Sykes, a frequent visitor in his roles as editor of *The Bulletin* and later, *Australian Business*. 'There wasn't much flashness about Consolidated Press, as you'll remember ... He liked it because he knew where he was, he had his car parked right across the road. It just suited him.'

'What you normally saw first of Packer were the soles of his feet—because he had his feet up on the desk, he was leaning back on the chair. Yep, feet on the desk. He was always relaxed. Unless he wasn't.'

Of course, such was the physical presence, the reputation and the sheer aura of Kerry Packer, he could have pontificated from a play-pit of Lego blocks. He was known to have advisers trail him around a golf course, and his executives naturally dropped everything to go wherever they were summoned.

The most unimaginable visits ever made to KP's office were two that occurred while he wasn't there. During the night of

28 April 1995, a person or persons managed to evade the Park Street alarm systems, sidestep security personnel and make their way directly to Packer's seat of power on the third floor.

Their aim was eerily precise, for they went to his personal safe, hidden within the drinks cabinet, and spent an estimated 30 minutes blow-torching the 1940s-vintage Chubb unit. The thief or thieves made off with a staggering $5.3 million in gold ingots. And staggering the crooks must have been; the 25 gold bars amounted to 285 kilograms. They also filched a jar of gold nuggets, plus gold and silver necklaces.

Park Street's security guards were obviously questioned. *Bulletin* cartoonist Patrick Cook remembers: 'The security guards were not, frankly, Rhodes scholars. When I went back into the office, there was a completely different outfit running security. The others had been rissoled on the spot. Small brown smears.'

The crime remains unsolved.

Almost eight years later, on 16 January 2003, a pair of armed bandits gained entry to Packer's office, tying up a member of the late-night cleaning staff. They, too, seem to have spent minimal time in going straight to Packer's top drawer and stealing his 9 millionm Glock pistol.

The gun was licensed, but Police were undecided on whether to charge Packer for failing to properly secure the weapon.

Packer voluntarily surrendered his pistol licence the following month, when it expired anyway. Perhaps he'd finally worked out he didn't need a side-arm in his office.

THE PACKERPHONE

Packer's ingested his news from watching television and talking to people. It was extraordinary for a businessman of his stature to do both for hours on end. Long conversations were Packer's information lifeline. They were a luxury afforded by his ownership of the nation's most news-centric commercial television network, and the most venerated weekly

'He was six foot three—always looked a bit taller—and very broad with it, and no minister of the government ever wanted to have Kerry personally in his office and thumping the desk and yelling at him. It was his personality. He could be quite intimidating and he knew how to be.'

TREVOR SYKES, FORMER EDITOR, *THE BULLETIN*

'Trevor Kennedy once said, "It's not the amount of money you spend that gives you influence. It's the amount of psychic stress you can give someone." And Kerry was a past master at that.'

Trevor Sykes, former editor, *The Bulletin*

'Anyone else care to beard the lion in his den?'

Kerry Packer, after dressing down an executive in his office.
—former ACP magazine executive

'I remember once we were at Palm Beach, me and my girlfriend sitting there on the sand. Mr Packer came down and said, "Good morning Andrew. Wouldn't be dead for quids, would you?" And I was amazed that even out of context, he'd remember who you were.'

ANDREW COWELL

'Packer is in Bermuda at some joint where they teach you to stop smoking. His horse is running in the Derby at Randwick on Easter Monday. So he calls in and gets Darrell Eastlake, who wouldn't know a horse from a cow.

"Kerry Packer here − how'd Easter go?"

"Oh, good, thanks Mr Packer. I had a surf and took the kids ..."

"Not that bloody Easter, you idiot, my horse Easter. The Derby."

Big Dazza's flying around ... searching for the results − Easter, sadly, flopped. Before hanging up, a gruff Packer says: "Who am I talking to?"

"Ian Maurice," Eastlake says, and hangs up.'

STEVE CRAWLEY, REPORTING ON A PHONE CALL RECEIVED AT NINE'S SPORTS PROGRAMMING OFFICE IN SYDNEY. EASTER, WINNER OF THE 1985 SPRING CHAMPION STAKES, WAS JOINTLY OWNED BY PACKER AND TRAINER, TOMMY SMITH. *THE BULLETIN*

'Tapp and I had only been on air for about 15 seconds when the phone rang at the Nine switchboard and a barking Kerry Packer said to the girl: "Tell that Tapp to put a tie on."

'Back after the next race Tapp still had his safari suit on with the open-neck shirt. "Tell Tapp he will be calling camel races in the Sahara if he hasn't got a tie on in a minute."

'After another ad break we came back and Tapp still had on his open-neck shirt. The phone rang again, but this time the switchboard lady was ready. Before the boss could speak she shouted: "Mr Packer, Mr Packer, they recorded this show at 10 o'clock this morning!"'

KEN CALLANDER, *GOOD LUCK AND GOOD PUNTING*

news magazine, not to mention his other business, sports and technology titles.

Packer could simply pick up the telephone at any time of the day or night and usually ask the newsmakers themselves.

And he did … literally at any time of the day or night. Executives knew they were effectively on call 24/7, and Packer had a positive genius (whose embodiment, from 1974–92, was his secretary Pat Wheatley) for tracking them down, anywhere on the globe.

In Park Street and the separate Nine Network executive office, a technology not universally understood in the 1970–80s allowed the Big Fella's telephone to simply override any other live call on the recipient's yellow 'Packerphone'. One editor could be in the middle of a conversation with another editor, and suddenly have the chairman there instead.

'I've always thought that having a boss who's interested in your work is decidedly better than having one who's not. He was clearly interested in our work, those of us who commentated on cricket, because we all got phone calls, but they were never phone calls that praised our work. He had a point to make.'

Tony Greig, to Martin Blake, 'This Sporting Life', *The Age*, 28 December 2005

Packer's style was hands-on and Benaud recalled that the console in the commentary box used to have a couple of orange lights on it that indicated when KP was calling. 'When those orange lights lit up, you knew there was a problem. Just occasionally it might be, "Tell so-and-so that was absolutely brilliant commentary. Can we have more along those lines? Can they explain it?" Generally it was, "What the hell's going on? What graphic was that?". I said to Hilly [executive producer, David Hill] one day, "We must be going pretty well. We don't seem to have had any orange lights." Then he said, "Just a moment." He dug down to his briefcase and pulled out two orange globes!'

Martin Blake, 'This Sporting Life', *The Age*, 28 December 2005

'You could never put anything past him. If you'd said something to him last month or the month before, and you tried to bullshit him about it instead of saying 'I forgot' – he'd say, 'What you said was this ...' Memory like a clam, I tell you. I thought, for a man doing everything he's doing, to remember all the little things like that ...'

KEVIN BARTLETT, RACING DRIVER AND KERRY PACKER'S CAR CONFIDANT

2

KERRYVISION

Frank Packer's two sons were disparate characters. Clyde was urbane and intellectual, with a growing curiosity of the alternative culture around him, while Kerry—dyslexic, an academic failure, quick with his fists—seemed destined to be useful mainly for lifting heavy things. In 1960, Clyde was editor-in-chief of *The Observer* magazine, while Kerry laboured in the basement among the printing presses of his father's cherished *Daily Telegraph* newspaper.

That same year, Sir Frank made the landmark acquisition of the GTV-9 television station in Melbourne. It would join his TCN-9 in Sydney, the station that had introduced television to Australia in 1956, and thus make the Packers unquestionably the most powerful people in TV.

Unsurprisingly, it was Clyde who was steered towards the television business. By 1970, he was joint managing director. The problem was that the other joint was his father. Their relationship exploded in 1972 when Sir Frank, never shy in using his media interests to express his political beliefs, forbade Nine's *A Current Affair* from airing an interview with then-ACTU president, Bob Hawke.

Clyde's subsequent departure in 1976 from Australia—and with it, the sale of his one-eighth share of the family business to Kerry for $4 million—sealed the future direction for Kerry Packer. But in fact, Kerry Packer had initiated the process a few years earlier.

'If you think
there's no
difference
between being
number one and
number two
in a fucking
two-station
market, then
you be fucking
number two.'

Kerry Packer to rival Ten boss Steve Cosser in 1990, responding to Cosser's
mooted plan to merge Ten and Seven to tackle Nine's dominance. Quoted in
The Rise and Rise of Kerry Packer -

In 1972, while Clyde was clashing with their father, Kerry was starting his bold and spectacularly successful magazine venture with *Cleo*. But for several years already, his goal had been to rid the business of the *Daily Telegraph* and *Sunday Telegraph* newspapers—a masthead his father had acquired in 1936.

Sir Frank's ailing health opened the door enough for Kerry to get his wish in May 1972. He and Rupert Murdoch had attended a boxing match together in Sydney and, sat in the car afterwards outside Murdoch's hotel, discussed various means of merging their respective morning (*Daily Telegraph*) and afternoon (*Mirror*) papers to compete with Fairfax's *Sydney Morning Herald* and *Sun*.

They agreed instead that Murdoch could buy the two *Telegraph* titles for $15 million. As the papers had regularly lost money, the deal was too good for even sentimental Sir Frank to refuse.

Beyond the state of the *Telegraph* titles, Kerry believed that newspapers themselves were yesterday's news. He would say as much in a 1977 interview with Murdoch's newspaper, *The Australian*:

'To be perfectly honest with you, I think that you people who are involved in print media don't quite understand that you are now the second-class media … your influence is nowhere near as great as the broadcast media.'

The interviewer asked: 'Your father would never have agreed with that?'

'No, of course he didn't. But you see one of the greatnesses about my father was the fact that emotionally, the last thing in the world he wanted to do was to sell the *Daily Telegraph*. It tore him to shreds. But he stood back from it as a businessman and said 'It's a good deal' and I was pushing him all the time to sell.'

Kerry Packer and television were made for each other.

He watched hours and hours of television each day—and, as many Nine employees would learn, at any hour of the night. One visitor to Packer's Bellevue Hill home in the late 1970s told of Packer watching four televisions simultaneously; the advent of split-screen monitors must have been a godsend.

Employees paint a picture of Packer as Nine's editor-in-chief, a one-man quality control department who—despite running magazine, rural, property and whatever other businesses—seemed magically able to perform this job 24 hours a day.

The image of an autocratic proprietor in the radiation haze of several television monitors, barking 'get that shit off the air!' down the telephone, seems quaint in today's era of media empires owned by faceless pension funds.

Packer's influence on television would not be limited to his own network—though most agree that the quality he demanded, and received, from his own stations, set the standard for rival networks. Like his father, Kerry did not hesitate to use political influence to further his business interests.

In many landmark examples, Packer was an undisputed winner, to an extent that even the impartiality of Prime Ministers was called into question.

It was Packer who, in August 1977, first approached Prime Minister Malcolm Fraser to invest in a satellite for national television broadcasting. In turn, the 1985 launch of AUSSAT would lead to the overhauling of 'two-station' ownership restrictions and their replacement, in 1986 by the government of Bob Hawke, with new 'cross-media' ownership laws.

Packer had been instrumental in their drafting, and it was more than happy coincidence that the cross-media restrictions pertained more to the proprietors of newspaper and radio than to magazine barons.

National-network potential made existing two-station networks incredibly hot property, and Packer's two Nines were the hottest. Thus would play out the biggest and best-known of Packer's incredible business deals, the selling—and relatively prompt re-acquisition—of Nine to Alan Bond, for $1.055 billion. Kerry Packer famously said you only get one Alan Bond in your lifetime.

Into the 1990s, Packer was no less active in lobbying for terrestrial stations to be given a ten-year head start in the

'TAKE THAT SHIT OFF THE AIR.'

Kerry Packer on the phone to long-serving Nine managing director, David Leckie, five minutes into the September, 1992 debut screening of *Australia's Naughtiest Home Videos*, hosted by Doug Mulray. The hour-long program continued for 25 minutes while Leckie argued back 'through several increasingly ferocious phone calls', according to Gerald Stone. Eventually, Packer phoned directly to Nine's control room and had it shut down. Leckie offered his resignation the next day, which Packer refused to accept. Leckie remained at Nine for another ten years.

'Well, when you get a television station we'll take notice of what you say.'

Kerry Packer's response to a journalist's criticism. *Four Corners*, ABC TV

'By the time I've got through the day I've done all my talking, all my mixing with people, done all the talking I want to do. For sanity reasons I can think of nothing better than lying down and watching television. Some people like to spend money on opera and ballet. I like doing things the average Australian likes—watching sport, going home and watching television.'

Kerry Packer quoted by Christopher Forsyth, *The Great Cricket Hijack*

'Once, during my tenure as executive producer of *60 Minutes*, I remember getting into a shouting match with him over his criticisms of a George Negus interview.

"Anyway, what am I supposed to do," I protested. "I've got four million viewers and you're only one of them!" There was a long, pregnant pause, giving me plenty of time to think about making out my application for the dole queue.

"I would have thought," he finally responded, "I would have at least counted for two."'

GERALD STONE, *THE BULLETIN*

KERRY: ... I just wanted to tell you that I've sold Channel 9.

[DAVID] HILL: Why the fuck!

KERRY: I sold it for more than a billion.

HILL: Who to?

KERRY: Alan Bond.

HILL: Aw, fuck!

KERRY: I just wanted to let you know ...

David Hill, head of sports at Nine, related the above exchange to Gerald Stone. Crucially, Hill added: 'And then his voice broke and he hung up.'
Gerald Stone, *Compulsive Viewing*

'Everyone underestimated him, including Frank. He understood television better than anyone else, and he understood what the average punter wanted: they wanted sport. And funnily enough, he related to the average punter better than to the toffs in the eastern suburbs. He knew they wanted sport, they wanted it live, they wanted it exciting.'

GREG CHAPPELL

new, digital television technology. He was early into the pay-TV game in a joint venture with Optus Vision, while Rupert Murdoch would team with Telstra. In 1998, Packer would acquire 25 per cent of Murdoch's Foxtel in the fallout from Super League.

Also in 1998, Nine embraced the worldwide web, buddying up with software giant Microsoft to establish Ninemsn and buy itself some time trying to figure out how to make money from the internet. Just like everyone, including Ninemsn, is *still* trying to figure it out.

Close observers of the television industry insist that Packer's failing health and his death in December 2005 was the end of a golden era for Nine. Such a view was certainly reflected in the station's ratings, and in the publicly embarrassing ructions among high-profile staff that regularly reached mainstream news.

To quote approximately everyone: That wouldn't have happened if Kerry were still in the chair.

'Kerry had great vision for what he wanted the network to be, number one was his prime ambition. He also had this desire to be the best at whatever we did. He wanted to be the best in sport, he wanted to be the best in entertainment, he wanted to be the best in news and current affairs.'

Lynton Taylor, former Nine and PBL executive, *Australian Story*, ABC TV

'I had one conversation with him in the first year of World Series Cricket, there was a lot of talk about how much money he was losing, he was going to go broke and all this. We were at the Chateau Commodore Hotel in Kings Cross, having a drink in the bar, and I said to him, "I read these stories ..." He said, "Son, they've got no idea. They don't understand television." And I can't remember the figures, but he said something like: "I've got to have *x*-amount of Australian content on the channel. Live sport is the cheapest content that I can put on. If I we're having to run a soapie, it would cost me five times as much. Son, this isn't costing me money—it's *making* me money."'

GREG CHAPPELL

'I have to say, in my 30 years at Nine I was never aware of any news story being dumped—or even being rewritten—because someone feared a commercial sponsor's complaint. Not even when, at *60 Minutes*, we "fingered" BHP for the Appin Coal Mine disaster. BHP, remember, was the major sponsor of *60 Minutes* – to the tune of over five million dollars a year.'

Ray Martin, 2008 ABC Sydney Andrew Olle Media Lecture

'Covering the Asian tsunami, as a news event, cost Kerry Packer three million precious dollars. Kerry wrote what was for him a rare "hero-gram" to the two blokes who spent all his money—David Gyngell and the news boss at the time, Max Uechtritz. He told them how proud he was of Nine's news coverage. He never mentioned the three million.'

Ray Martin, 2008 ABC Sydney Andrew Olle Media Lecture

'Saturday was usually an all-nighter for the program's executive producer Alan Hogan and the film editors. The editing process was fuelled by cigarettes, coffee and more than the odd tube of cold beer. We arrived one morning to find Hogan in a state of near-shock. In the early hours of the morning—around three o'clock—while engrossed in the editing process, he felt an additional presence in the darkened editing suite. There, looming in the gloom was Kerry Packer, who explained he had dropped across to see how the program was put together. According to Hogan, Kerry stayed for around an hour as the editing process was explained. Then he disappeared into the night ...'

MAX WALSH, FOUNDING PRESENTER OF *SUNDAY* ON THE NINE NETWORK, *THE BULLETIN*

'Two hours of largely live TV production was emotionally draining, but as we returned to the *Sunday* cottage for a leisurely post-mortem we learned that was not all. Kerry Packer was on the telephone line with what turned out to be his extended critique, not only of the program but of the whole Falklands War. Initially we were flattered that Kerry Packer was taking such a close interest. But that turned out to be a mixed blessing in the weeks ahead. Those *Sunday* phone calls became a game of pass the parcel.'

Max Walsh, founding presenter of *Sunday* on the Nine Network, *The Bulletin*

'Kerry was both a lifelong friend and a tough competitor. He was the most successful businessman of our generation. As a broadcaster, he had an uncanny knack of knowing what people across the country were thinking and this finely-tuned antenna made him the best broadcaster the country has seen.'

RUPERT MURDOCH

As head of sport, David Hill remembers being on duty late one night during a nightmarish broadcast in which the satellite kept dropping out, spoiling coverage of a major British golf tournament. At 2.30am, a great hulk suddenly loomed up behind him in the gloom of studio control.

'Kerry, what are you doing here?' Hill asked in alarm.

'I think this might arguably be the greatest disaster in the history of television,' Packer chided. 'I just wanted to watch it up close.'

Gerald Stone, *The Bulletin*, 4 January 2006, from a story originally told in *Compulsive Viewing*

'Packer was such a great television proprietor when it came to sporting telecasts because he was the number one sporting viewer in Australia himself. He loved sport and he loved television, and he knew about both of them ... The ludicrous situation in 2007 where Channel Ten finished a day's telecast of the US Masters with Tiger Woods on the seventeenth tee with two holes to play would not have occurred if Nine still had the telecast. Packer would have been watching, and he would not have let it happen.'

KEN CALLANDER, *GOOD LUCK AND GOOD PUNTING*

WORLD SERIES CRICKET

In the mid-1970s, Australian cricket was bowling up a high-speed catwalk of tousle-haired wild boys, oozing larrikin humour and hard-playing, hairy-chested sex appeal. The one thing they couldn't compete with was the national average wage. These were world-class athletes, yet none could afford to do it professionally.

The dynamic between the players and the sport's governors, the Australian Cricket Board (ACB), was well illustrated in 1974 when the players made a request for higher pay. The ACB responded with a stern reminder that it, the ACB, was bestowing upon them the honour of representing their country. If the players didn't like it, there were hundreds in line behind them.

Meanwhile, cricket itself was in danger of losing relevance to a generation of younger television viewers. To all but the converted, it was of only small consolation that, from 1975, about 80 per cent of the evident action in a test cricket telecast—the photosynthesis of lawn—was now occurring in colour.

Emboldened by his breakthrough marketing and broadcasting of the Australian Open Golf tournament in 1975, Packer set his sights on cricket. He would re-package the game's energy and appeal for the era of colour television, and ensure that the players earned a living more appropriate to their status as national heroes.

From the very introduction of television to Australia in 1956, televising of the game had been effectively a gentleman's-club agreement between the ACB and the Australian Broadcasting Commission. The cricket authorities used the television-rights income to feed back into the game at all its amateur levels. The ABC cultivated its cardigan-collecting cricket audience with a practical monopoly on televising the game. The ABC's rights were non-exclusive, but every other network knew that it faced a national broadcaster that did not need to interrupt its programming with commercials.

Packer's initial play was straightforward enough. In early 1976, he approached the cricket board with a bid for *exclusive* broadcast rights for the national Sheffield Shield and

'THERE'S A LITTLE BIT OF THE WHORE IN ALL OF US. GENTLEMEN, NAME YOUR PRICE.'

Kerry Packer to Ray Steele of the Australian Cricket Board, during the 1976 negotiations for television broadcast rights. Steele's recollection was that Packer said: 'We're all harlots, how much do you want?'

'It would be easier to get an audience with the Pope. And I'm not a Catholic.'

KP, ON HIS CHANCES OF MEETING WITH THE AUSTRALIAN CRICKET BOARD, AFTER WORLD SERIES CRICKET'S 1977 VICTORY IN THE ENGLISH HIGH COURT OF JUSTICE, AS TOLD IN *HOWZAT! KERRY PACKER'S WAR*, CHRISTOPHER LEE

'Cricket is going to get revolutionised whether they like it or not. There is nothing they can do to stop me. Not a goddamned thing.'

Kerry Packer to the Australian media, May 1977

international Test cricket matches. At a Melbourne meeting in June, Packer offered $1.5 million over three years.

The ACB's weak response was that, oh dear, he was too late; they'd made a verbal (if not contractual) agreement with the ABC, and in any event, *exclusive* rights just weren't on.

Packer knew that the ABC offer, at $207,000 for three years, should have been obliterated. He sensed mere mule-headedness. Plenty have speculated that the ACB's response inflamed the Packer anti-establishment gene.

Packer, famously, suggested that all in the room shared an even more deeply-rooted gene; one dating back to the most ancient profession. ACB negotiator Ray Steel remembers the line as: 'We're all harlots, how much do you want?').

But Kerry Packer got no play from the game's governors. The meeting was dismissed, Packer left wondering why the hell these men—with the full knowledge of his intentions—had made him bother to fly down to Melbourne in the first place.

Unbeknown to Packer, at around that very time, the spark for his revenge was being fanned beneath an ill-fitting surf life-saver's cap. John Cornell was a former producer on *A Current Affair*. Cornell was now managing the stellar career of his comedian mate Paul Hogan, and doubling as Hoges' dim-witted sidekick, Strop. In early 1976, Cornell was approached by friend and former Perth footballer Austin 'Ocker' Robertson to manage fellow Perth sportsman, cricketer Dennis Lillee.

In *Howzat! Kerry Packer's War*, Cornell recalled asking Lillee for a list of his earnings. For nine months of playing cricket, the moustachioed sex symbol had trousered less than $9000. He made most of his living selling cars for a Perth dealership.

Cornell was astonished. 'I can get [$9000] for two nights' entertainment from Hoges,' he thought. 'The players [are] getting ripped off.'

The figures proved that they were. Back in August 1975, witnessing escalating sponsorship from tobacco giant Amatil, Australia's outspoken captain Ian Chappell had met with cricket authorities in Sydney and again put forward the case for a pay rise.

Gideon Haigh's *The Cricket War: The Inside Story of Kerry Packer's World Series* revealed that, up to this point, the Australia players had received $200 to play a Test match, plus $50 expenses and $35 for meals away from home. Chappell's initiative had at least resulted in these sums being roughly doubled for the 1975–76 season.

Cornell and Hogan, under their banner JP Productions, formulated the idea of special, made-for-TV exhibition matches to generate some extra income for the players outside their Shield and Test calendar. Lillee—and in short order, the recently retired Ian Chappell—assured them the idea would be a hit with the players.

But both also insisted that the ACB should be left well out of it.

What Cornell needed was a television proprietor. As a bonus, he found one with a fresh chip on his shoulder the size of the Australian Cricket Board.

The serendipity was not lost on the Big Fella. Neither was the already brilliant Cornell-Hogan hatching beyond immediate improvement. Packer proposed that they take it farther than Australians playing each other. 'Let's get the world's best cricketers to play Australia's best."

A world series for cricket.

With Lillee and Chappell doing the recruiting, Richie Benaud doing the schmoozing, and the base rate for players set at a staggering $25,000 per year for a three-year contract, the maverick series had signed up 35 of the world's best players in complete secrecy before news of it finally escaped in May, 1977.

Cue the sound of smashing brandy snifters. And the *pffft!* of a fuck-you Fanta.

For many people, Australians included, their first real consciousness of Kerry Packer came via his appearance on *The Frost Programme* in the UK on 2 June 1977. Interviewer David Frost—who already knew Packer well—had pitted the cricket-promoting pariah against *Sunday Times* cricket writer Robin Marlar.

'Those people have all given long service to cricket. I believe they're entitled to make a decent living out of it. They are the lowest-paid team sport practically in the world. Why shouldn't they earn more money?'

Kerry Packer on *The Frost Programme*, 2 June 1977

'It's the easiest sport in the world to take over. Nobody bothered to pay the players what they were worth.'

KERRY PACKER

'Jesus son, it's almost bright enough to play cricket...'

KP to John Cornell in May, 1977, at VFL Park in Melbourne, where they'd gone to inspect the playing field for its (marginal) suitability for cricket. It was early evening, and the floodlit field provided the eureka moment for night cricket. Quoted in *Howzat! Kerry Packer's War*

[Nine head of sports] David Hill's coverage of Packer's beloved cricket brought out Kerry at his best and worst. During Test matches he was constantly on the phone, complaining about anything from a shaky camera shot to an umpire's decision. 'He wasn't out!' he would shout to a bemused Hill, who could hardly have done anything about it.

Sydney Morning Herald, 31 December 2005

'So often did Kerry phone in [to David Hill] to offer advice on some aspect of cricket coverage that Hill even got a call from him at the Gabba in Brisbane just to let him know he would be playing golf that day.

"Oh, that's nice," the harassed producer interrupted, "but why are you telling me?"

"I didn't want you to think I was sick," Kerry replied.'

GERALD STONE, *THE BULLETIN*

'So we take a loss of $2 million. So what? I couldn't buy all that top television time, 315 hours of it, for one million dollars, so that cuts the loss to a million. After tax it's $500,000. Am I going to suffer fits of apoplexia at night worrying about half a million dollars?'

Kerry Packer to Phillip Cornford of *The Australian*, November 1977, on the loss-making first season of WSC. *Howzat! Kerry Packer's War*

It was the Aussie upstart versus the establishment toff. Packer, far from being coarse and bullying, was ice-cool and confident with his quips, while Marlar escalated to a spit-soaked fundamentalist. The interview ended with the audience cheering for cricket's 'super-test' to go ahead.

Naturally, many Brits saw it differently. 'The circus may last a season or two—there are good reasons for thinking that it will be no longer than that—and it may do much harm to the game,' sniffed Britain's *The Spectator* on 10 June 1977.

Packer's poke at a world series would have to go all the way to England's High Court. In September 1977, the attempt by the International Cricket Conference (aka 'the establishment') to ban Packer-aligned players from the game was defeated. The ICC's tilt at Kerry Packer reportedly ended up costing $320,000.

If anyone had thought rounding up (eventually) 51 of the world's top cricketers would be Packer's biggest challenge, there were still greater obstacles ahead.

Packer's 'circus' was frozen out from those cricket grounds administered by the Australian cricket authorities. It was forced to look at other sporting venues like Melbourne's VFL Park where, compared with the manicured nuances of a cricket pitch, the surface was an Amazonian jungle.

Expert horticulturalists were engaged to cultivate cricket pitches off-site in huge concrete trays, to be trucked into place. Even then, the final few metres of their journey would require steel plates to protect the surrounding grass from the weight of the vehicles.

It was during an evening inspection of VFL Park, where footballers were training on the floodlit field, that Packer and Cornell hit on the idea of night cricket. Putting this into practice, however, would necessitate the design and construction of lighting towers for the other venues, including the Sydney Showground. Night cricket even meant changing the colour of the ball.

With every brainstorm, cricket traditionalists bristled.

It's a matter of history that in its first season, World Series Cricket looked like it would crater. Packer had revealed during the High Court case that he had committed to investing $12 million into the game. Yet everyone could see, live on Packer TV, that the first matches were struggling to pull in a few thousand spectators each.

The face of cricket *was* changing. The television coverage was in a different league, with cameras at both ends of the pitch, and eight cameras in total to relay unprecedented detail. So, too, the field microphones that were buried near the stumps, protected from the damp earth by being stuffed inside condoms.

At the second Supertest, played at the Sydney Showground, David Hookes's jaw was shattered by a ball from the West Indian bowler. Seeing the severity of the injury, Packer personally bundled Hookes into his Jaguar sedan and raced him the kilometre or so to St Vincent's Hospital.

Strangely, Hookes' misfortune sent a powerful message to cricket fans: WSC wasn't playing pretendies. Another consequence was that batsman's helmets would soon become commonplace in cricket.

In those countries where cricket is played, the argy-bargy continued over whether Packer signatories should be allowed on their national teams. The West Indies lifted its ban, then Pakistan, but England and Australia remained firmly opposed. The Australian WSC side was still forbidden from being called 'Australia'.

The turning point for WSC occurred at VFL Park in Melbourne in late January 1978, as the first season drew to a close. Its first night game, a limited (40-over) match between the Australians and the World side in December, had still only drawn a modest crowd of about 6500. But the concept of city commuters meeting their families after work to watch an evening of cricket became etched in the public's minds.

When the night game returned to VFL Park in January, almost four times as many spectators turned up. Similar turnouts over the following two nights' play confirmed that World Series Cricket had indeed, to quote *Cricketer* magazine editor Eric Beecher, 'turned on the lights'.

'It's had a hundred years' practice. If it's not ready now it'll never be.'

Kerry Packer on *The Frost Programme* on 2 June 1977, responding to *Sunday Times* cricket writer Robin Marlar's assertion that the cricket establishment was 'not equipped to withstand this kind of business piracy'

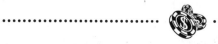

'Do you think this is a democracy? I'm paying the money, you're the fucking captain'

Kerry Packer to Ian Chappell, at their first meeting to discuss the WSC. Ian had gently pointed out that his brother Greg was captain of Australia at the time

'I am only in the arena because of my disagreement with the Australian Cricket Board. Had I got those TV rights I was prepared to withdraw from the scene and leave the running of cricket to the Board. I will not take steps to help anyone. It's every man for himself and the Devil take the hindmost.'

KERRY PACKER, AFTER BEING TOLD ON 23 JUNE 1977 OF THE INTERNATIONAL CRICKET CONFERENCE'S DECISION TO WITHHOLD EXCLUSIVE TELEVISION RIGHTS

'I think the two greatest influences in the last 100 years of Australian cricket have been Sir Donald Bradman and Kerry Packer.'

Bob Merriman, Cricket Australia chairman 2001–05, speaking in May 2005 on Cricket Australia's centenary

'All the commentators in World Series Cricket had navy blue jackets with a Channel Nine logo of some kind on them. This was back in 1977–78. Kerry Packer rang up and said to the producer: "Tell Richie to get a light-coloured jacket, I want him to be different so people know he's a presenter. All the others continue on with their navy jacket." I kept the navy jacket as well, but the first one was a light grey and then it varied over the years until it came into a beige.'

Former cricketer and legendary Nine commentator Richie Benaud on the origin of his trademark 'cream' jacket. 'Marvellous that, Richie gets better with beige', *Sydney Morning Herald*, 22 November 2009

In the second year of the league, Australia were about to leave for a tour of the Caribbean ... [Ian] Chappell, Australia's captain, was called in to Packer's Park Street headquarters in Sydney, where Packer asked if he was happy with his team, and it emerged that the sum of $16,000 was less than the daily rate stipulated under the WSC contract.

Packer turned to Lynton Taylor, his executive, and said, "Aren't we paying according to the contract?"

Taylor replied: "No, Kerry, but Ian's sorted it out with the players. It's all fixed ..."

Chappell interjected: "This is ridiculous, Kerry. You're not going to make any money out of this tour to the Caribbean. Our blokes are going to make more money on this tour than they'd earn at home."

But Packer was determined. He turned to Taylor. "How much more would it cost if we pay according to the contract?"

Taylor did his sums quickly and replied: "About $340,000 ..."

"Son, I'll tell you something," [Packer] said to Chappelli. "$340,000 is about the price of a B-grade movie for my TV station. That's not going to break me. What will fucking-well break me is not sticking to the word of my contracts. Lynton, pay 'em."

ASHLEY MALLETT, 'WHAT KERRY DID', ESPN SPORTS MEDIA

There was no stopping WSC after that, especially with its weapon for the 1978–79 season: a television jingle turned sporting national anthem, *C'mon Aussie c'mon*. Its authors: Allan Johnston and the late Alan Morris, of Sydney agency Mojo.

As World Series Cricket grew in spectacle, urgency and colour (with the 'pyjama' uniforms introduced in January 1979), its crowd figures rocketed. The Supertest final of the 1978–79 season, played under the Packer-prompted (and controversially, State-funded) lighting towers of the Sydney Cricket Ground, drew 40,000 spectators over three days.

The 'official' Australia-versus-England Test was hosted at the very same venue just one week later. It attracted a crowd of just 22,000, over four days. Packer's gut-punch to the ACB had truly hit home.

And WSC wasn't just great sport—it was spectacularly good television business. According to Nine's annual report for 1978-79:

'Cricket added one point each hour of broadcast towards Nine's Australian content quota whilst drawing between half and three quarters of the available audience. Tests and One-Day Internationals have won their slots 99 per cent of the time. A mini-series that received similar ratings would cost around 80 times as much to produce and even a cheap "soap" costs some 16 times as much.'

Outside of Packer's orbit, it seemed, cricket was heading into a flat spin. Australia's Test performances were suffering for the absence of the top-line players and crowd attendances at Tests were plummeting. With them went the ACB's revenues, even in the face of increasing sponsorship from tobacco giant, Amatil.

In the end, in May 1979—just two years after the cricket world first heard of Packer, the pariah—the warring sides agreed to a truce. What emerged in time for the 1979–80 cricket season was a sort of hybrid of the two factions, bringing together the players, marketing ploys, one-day and night-time matches and a vastly upgraded standard of television broadcasting of the game.

On Packer's Nine network, naturally. Live and exclusive.

'At Waverley Park, during the first year of WSC, we were playing a day-night game against the West Indies. The lights had to be turned off at 10pm ... Kerry decided it was too good to stop early. The umpires were informed, the West Indies were informed, but we weren't informed. We subsequently lost the match ...

'Ian, as captain, was really upset. Andrew Caro [WSC managing director] walked into the dressing room, put his hand on Ian's shoulder and said, "Bad luck son"—and Ian wheeled on him. He said, "There's no bad luck about it ... anyway, I don't know why I'm talking to the monkey—get me the organ grinder!"

'Kerry appeared in the doorway a few minutes later ... he tapped Ian on the shoulder and said, "I believe we've got a problem, son?" And Ian turned around and said, "No, Kerry. *You've* got a problem ... You tell us about professionalism—well, you've got to be professional as well. This is an absolute f-up."

'Kerry said, "Son, don't worry about it, we'll give you the same money as the West Indies". And Ian said, "You can shove your money. We don't want your money, we want you to get organised. Now fuck off."

'Kerry reeled backwards. He obviously hadn't been spoken to like that too often. He started to say something, then realised it probably wasn't appropriate, and he turned and walked out the door.

'You could see from the look on his face, A: that it hadn't happened very often, and B: that it had hit home. To his credit, he did get it sorted out. Andrew went missing, Lynton Taylor took over and things did get in shape after that. We had no more problems.

'I think Ian telling him to fuck off was probably the first time he'd really just felt like one of the boys.'

GREG CHAPPELL

'I remember sitting up on the top deck with Kerry looking through binoculars counting, literally counting, the people coming through the turnstile: thirty-six, thirty-seven, thirty-eight ...'

David Evans, general manager of GTV9, on WSC's inauspicious first Supertest at VFL Park in 1977 in *Compulsive Viewing*

'Kerry Packer had more influence on big-time cricket than anybody who never held a bat. He dragged the game kicking and screaming into the 20th century and ensured its prosperity in the 21st. Cricketers were ill-served by their masters. The politest things that can be said about the establishment when Packer came along [were] that they were naïve, incompetent nincompoops.'

TONY GREIG, 'MY FRIEND KERRY', *THE WISDEN CRICKETER*

'Well, let's be honest. Kerry Packer and World Series Cricket did the game a favour ... If we had tried as a Board in 1979 to have persuaded the administrators throughout the country to play limited-overs cricket to the extent we now play it, with coloured clothing, white balls and the other things that went along with it, our chances of getting that to happen within a reasonable length of time would have been virtually nil ... Cricket owes Mr Packer. And I believe that sincerely.'

Bob Parish, former ACB chairman and stonewaller of Packer's WSC, quoted by Gerald Stone, *Compulsive Viewing*

'[Packer] has a very strong view on programming, that we should be giving everybody the opportunity to see good cricket. He sees cricket as entertainment and if it's not entertaining, he wants to do something about it. If the wicket's crook or the ball's crook, or he's not happy with the way the game's being played, he has a view ... He's concerned if the quality of cricket falls away.'

CRICKET AUSTRALIA CHAIRMAN BOB MERRIMAN, ON NINE'S EXTENDING ITS CRICKET COVERAGE FOR A FURTHER SEVEN YEARS.

'I don't want to fucking spend half a game looking at the fucking batsman's arse.'

Kerry Packer to executive producer David Hill

'They talk about not being able to pay the cricketers enough. They could have had my money to do it.'

KP's retort to the ACB's crying poor

Ashley Mallett was an off spinner and in [Ian] Chappell's opinion the best in the country, but Packer regarded Mallett as a 'straight-break' bowler and didn't want to sign him to his troupe. Chappell did a deal with his new employer. 'If Mallett can get you out in one over will you sign him to a contract?' Chappell asked Packer. 'He (Packer) said, "Yeah". He immediately started practising, that's how serious he was. He was a cricket fan. He loved talking about cricket and talking about sport. That was why it was a pleasure to work for him, because you knew he wasn't just a television magnate churning out product.'

MARTIN BLAKE, 'THIS SPORTING LIFE', *THE AGE*, 28 DECEMBER 2005

For two days I sweated it out, then [Ian Chappell] got back to me with an offer... of sorts.

"Kerry's willing to give you a contract, but only if you agree to fly to Sydney and bowl against him for one over. If you get him out twice in the six balls, he will make an offer for your services."

I did not hesitate: "Chappelli, tell Mr Packer to get fucked!"

I got a contract.

Some 30 years later, I asked Chappelli if he had relayed our conversation verbatim to KP. He said, "No, Rowd. I didn't think it would be in your best interests."

ASHLEY MALLETT, 'WHAT KERRY DID', 25 DECEMBER 2011, ESPN SPORTS MEDIA

'His contribution in the fullness of time is now recognised as being very beneficial to cricket. There were many at the time who wondered, but, there are now people who recognise that just the way in which one day cricket has transformed the game, it has brought new people to it, it has also, I believe, given all Test players new skills and it has enlivened Test cricket and it would be one of his very significant legacies.'

PRIME MINISTER JOHN HOWARD, PRESS CONFERENCE AT KIRRIBILLI HOUSE, 27 DECEMBER 2005

'While Australians will today be watching the cricket it should be said that Kerry Packer will be remembered with gratitude by Australian cricketers, as the man who brought just recompense for their skills in the professional game.'

Kim Beazley, Leader of the Opposition, media statement, 27 December 2005

'It does no harm for modern first class and international cricketers to sit back and assess why in 2006 their financial situations are so markedly different from 30 years ago. Kerry is the reason.'

RICHIE BENAUD, SPEAKING AT KERRY PACKER'S MEMORIAL SERVICE, SYDNEY, 17 FEBRUARY 2006

'From my short experiences with him, he came across as a pretty regular guy. He lived in very different circumstances from most of us, but he loved a punt, he loved his sport, he loved a night out. He was a regular bloke under it all ... I think he got a great thrill out of being around the [WSC players]. I think he took every opportunity to be around us—because I reckon it was the only time he was treated like one of the boys.'

GREG CHAPPELL

'Now there are certain things you do for the benefit of the country. The America's Cup is one. I would suggest to you that the Australian Open golf is another. I don't expect we will ever make money out of that.'

REFLECTING ON HIS FATHER SIR FRANK'S TILTS AT THE AMERICA'S CUP—A PURSUIT FOR WHICH KERRY HAD NEVER DISGUISED HIS CONTEMPT, *THE AUSTRALIAN*, 1975.

KP TO A TEE

Before World Series Cricket came smashing through our television screens, Kerry Packer could have been just another Australian media mogul. He was by no means the top Aussie media tycoon on people's minds at that time.

Rupert Murdoch was making headlines in the US through the mid-1970s, snapping up the *New York Post* newspaper and the magazine group publisher of *The Village Voice*. In January 1977, Murdoch was cartooned on the cover of *TIME*, a kangaroo King Kong flogging papers from New York's skyscrapers.

Murdoch's scale of operation would continue to outstrip Packer's, but their paths would be quite similar. And the rival scions who had, between them, negotiated the $15 million sale of the *Telegraph* in the back seat of a car in 1972, were destined to butt heads almost a quarter of a century later—on a sporting field.

Packer's offloading of the *Telegraph* titles was a case of Kerry fixing his eye on the ball. He had never cared for newspapers; he read them with difficulty, if at all. In television, Packer could play to his strengths.

Imagine making a career out of sitting in front of the telly, eating burgers, swigging one's preferred beverage and watching sport—cricket, golf, footy, whatever. For Packer, television and sport wasn't just a career, but a calling.

In following it, he would make millions. And along the way, make Nine a weekend institution for sports fans, revolutionise an entire game and change live sports broadcasting forever.

The tee shot occurred in 1975. In his own right, Packer was a more than capable golfer. At the Royal Sydney Golf Club, his name is listed as the winner of the 1965 Herbert Marks Trophy, and of the 1970 Royal Sydney Cup. At the time of the latter event, he played off a handicap of five. But he fell out with the Royal Sydney, in snooty Rose Bay, and took up at The Australian Golf Club, in slightly less salubrious Kensington, beneath the flight path of Sydney Airport.

The Australian Open is said to be the second oldest golf championship in the world (after The Open Championship in Scotland). It was first played in 1904, predating the US Masters at Augusta by 30 years. The Australian Open changed venues each year to take in courses around the nation, but in 1975 it was to be played where it had all begun 71 years earlier, at The Australian in Sydney.

Despite the jet-set image and the draw of golf's 'Big Three'— Gary Player, Jack Nicklaus and Arnold Palmer—the Australian Open was in the rough. In 1975, it was in desperate need of a title sponsor. Packer pitched in $1 million in prize money, under the banner of *The Bulletin*, and proposed that the then-Australian Golf Union, owner of the event, grant him television rights for three years.

But KP was already looking farther down the fairway. Jack Nicklaus had once referred to the Australian Open as the world's fifth major, putting it in lofty company with the venerable British and the three big US tournaments. Packer believed that a permanent home, as the US Masters enjoyed with Augusta, would cement the Open's prestige.

The AGU had been founded in 1898 in Melbourne. It reeked of southern-city Establishment, and bristled at Packer's Sydney-centric vision of the Open. But Packer tipped what was estimated as a further $2 million in the direction of Nicklaus, by then a budding course designer, to transform The Australian into a world-class course.

Packer streamlined the way in which players were paid, proposing a one-size-fits all payment (reportedly $6000 a head), plus air fares, accommodation and Packer-sized hospitality. Several were billeted at Cairnton, Packer's Bellevue Hill estate.

KP may have had good reason to keep a close eye on the invoices. He'd already figured on losing money on the Open. But in the end, he and the Nine team would learn lessons in live broadcasting that later proved priceless.

A network of buried cables, established during the wholesale redesign of the golf course, allowed for far more cameras than had been seen before; advertising and sponsorship

'The Yanks came out here to see our [Nine] coverage of the Australian Open golf tournament. For the first time anywhere, we covered all 18 holes and they went back home and started doing the same.'

KP to Ian Chappell, on their first meeting to discuss WSC. Ian Chappell, 'Kerry Packer's cricket revolution changed the way the game was played forever', *Daily Telegraph*, 19 August 2012

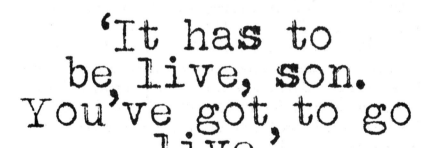

'It has to be live, son. You've got to go live.'

Kerry Packer to John Quayle, then general manager of the ARL, as told to *The Bulletin* (4 January 2006) 'It took it from being a detached coverage of a footy match, to a real show in its own right. And in prime time.'

'I would just like you to know that I have a binding contract with you people, and if any of the clubs go against it, I'll sue the arse off you.'

KERRY PACKER WARNING ARL CLUB BOSSES AGAINST JOINING SUPER LEAGUE AT A MEETING IN FEBRUARY 1995

Packer took Piggins to a hotel in Double Bay. Over a couple of lemon squashes the media mogul confessed he used to support the Bunnies. The conversation went something like this.

Piggins: So why haven't you given us any money?

Packer: You never asked.

Piggins: Consider yourself asked.

Packer: How much do you need?

Piggins: $3 million.

Packer: (Shaking his head) No.

Packer did, however, write a cheque for $750,000 on the spot.

'PIGGINS STILL THE PEOPLE'S VOICE', ADRIAN PROSZENKO, *SYDNEY MORNING HERALD*, 3 JULY 2011

opportunities expanded accordingly. With colour, drama and unprecedented detail, the telecast rated well. Nicklaus' victory (on the course he had designed) generated plenty of international publicity.

Indeed, Nicklaus would win three of the four Australian Opens played under Packer's patronage (Australia's David Graham foiled a hat-trick in 1977), after the original three-year deal was extended into 1978. For the duration, the AGU had shifted its headquarters to Sydney.

All of that would change quickly after the 1978 tournament, when the AGU insisted on a return to a Melbourne course for 1979. Packer, contemplating the scale of his investment in The Australian, was understandably miffed.

Packer had to walk away from the Australian Open, but he did not abandon The Australian Golf Club. Veteran golf writer Peter Stone, writing in *The Sydney Morning Herald*, estimated that, over the years, Packer personally contributed some $18 million to the ongoing benefit of the course.

Later it was reported that Kerry had also approached the Lawn Tennis Association of Australia with an offer of $1 million, to secure five years' television and marketing rights for the Australian Open tennis. The LTAA eventually turned it down, but it was a line call.

Many years after his WSC success, Packer would face one more major sporting stoush; a bodyline bowl at him, using the same world-series concept he had pioneered for cricket.

His rival was his media mogul 'frenemy', Rupert Murdoch.

The scuffle began in 1986, when the newly-empowered Australian Rugby League decided to begin paring down the gaggle of teams from the game's traditional heartland, Sydney. By 1994, the culling or merging of smaller Sydney clubs had opened the way for rugby league to expand its national footprint, starting with the 1995 season.

Packer owned the broadcast rights for rugby league, having inked a seven-year, $80 million deal in 1993. Significantly, the deal included both free-to-air and pay television, though the latter service was not yet available in Australia.

The power of pay TV certainly wasn't unknown to either tycoon. Murdoch's UK BSkyB satellite company—steered by Packer's former Nine lieutenant, Sam Chisholm—had built its financial turnaround largely on the back of English football. In Australia, Murdoch's Foxtel brand was gearing up for launch in 1995. Packer had a stake in the inevitable pay TV technology via Optus Vision.

Packer-powered football was already working magic on the game's popularity. Kerry insisted that the rugby league games be broadcast live. He knew what the fans wanted.

But not everyone was happy. Rumblings had begun in 1994 in Queensland about the teams' share of the $10 million-a-year television bounty. The Murdoch camp swung behind the Queensland Broncos, proposing a plan all too familiar to Packer: a 'super league' of players, in a made-for-cable championship.

Packer sought to stamp it out, warning club bosses that he would take legal action. A month later, though, a signing spree by Murdoch's men had bagged a handful of top coaches and about 30 players' signatures for the maverick series.

Murdoch could play as hard as Packer ever had. Wendell Sailor, then a star Broncos player, wrote in his autobiography *Crossing The Line*: 'We'd already been quietly warned that if we backed out of our Super League deals, News Ltd would sue us for everything we had and we would never play rugby league anywhere in the world ever again. The UK Rugby League had also signed up for Super League, so if we pissed these guys off, there was nowhere else to go.'

Sailor went on to add that his Super League contract, worth more than twice what he'd previously been paid, suddenly looked pale after a private meeting with James Packer and ARL coach (and KP confidante), Bob Fulton. The pockets of Nine and Optus Vision, sponsor of the 1996 premiership, were

'JESUS, THIS IS NOT A GOOD TIME TO GET HIM TO OPEN HIS WALLET, I THOUGHT.'

'I had a business meeting with him in Park Street, and it happened to be the actual day that Super League broke [early 1995]. And he was on the other side of it—he had the rights for Rugby League and Murdoch took it out from under him.

'I hadn't been to his office before, Pat Wheatley had a secretary—so I was greeted by the secretary of the secretary—and shown to the waiting room, alongside Kerry's office. I had a 12 o'clock appointment and I got there a bit early. I had a 10 or 15-minute presentation prepared in my head.

'Anyway, 12 o'clock comes and goes; 12:30 comes and goes; and I'm starting to get a bit agitated ... And then I hear Kerry's voice come into his office from the other entrance. All I could hear was Kerry: "You effin' said this, you said effin' that"—I subsequently found out he had his lawyers with him, and they'd been on the losing side.'

GREG CHAPPELL

deep. 'They were offering me a three-year contract, each year in the neighbourhood of half a million dollars,' Sailor wrote.

The battle hit the Federal Court in September 1995. After months of legal head-butting, it appeared that Packer had won the day: Super League would be banned until 2000, when Nine's contract was up. But an appeal lodged in May 1996 overturned it all. Suddenly, Murdoch's men were lacing up their studs for a 1997 Super League season.

Thus, 1997 was at best a Murdoch victory over Packer, at worst a tense and temporary co-habitation. At the conclusion of that sole season of Super League, the warring tribes gathered in Sydney Football Stadium—in the shadow of 'Packer's candles'—and voted to run the ball forward under a new partnership, the National Rugby League.

Many saw this compromise as a rare capitulation on Packer's part. If so, it was the kind he didn't mind, because the negotiation included Murdoch handing him 25 per cent of Foxtel, the pay-TV provider, and 50 per cent of the Fox Sports group of channels.

Nobody has doubted that it was a victory for the game.

3

BUSH YARNS

The storyline sounds simple enough: high-pressure city businessman has a health scare in his mid-40s, decides on a tree-change, buys a remote little rural bolt-hole. For irrepressible business people of Kerry Packer's ilk, however, it's always just a short hop from here to creating the nation's second-largest pastoral empire, running 350,000 head of cattle on 19 stations covering 5.8 million hectares.

Sir Frank Packer had bought the first piece of land at Ellerston in 1972, doing so jointly with wool-broker, James McLeod. The two men had shared ownership of two adjoining properties since 1956.

Ellerston was bought to expand their wool and cattle interests, but both men had been keen polo players. In 1938, they were among the five co-founders of the Town and Country Polo Club. Sir Frank had also served on the committee of the NSW Polo Association.

While Sir Frank was alive, the original 40,500 hectares was gradually pared off to just 9,000 hectares. But in the 10 years following his death in 1974, Kerry built it up again, acquiring neighbouring properties to reach a total of more than 27,000 hectares. Ellerston was a working station running up to 11,000 Hereford cattle and 6,500 Merino wethers.

Gretel Packer reflected that her father's sense of home at Ellerston ran deep. 'Dad really loved Ellerston,' she told *The Australian Women's Weekly* in February 2006. 'In the early

'I own more cattle than anyone else in the world. I own more land than any man in Australia. Why can't I get a decent fucking steak in my own house?'

Kerry Packer, as told by Alan Jones, *The Bulletin*, 4 January 2006

days, it was primarily a cattle and sheep property. When he was younger, Dad would go up there and be like a lot of men in their 30s and 40s, filled with energy and enthusiasm to go riding and shooting.'

It was Bondy's billion that set off Packer's spending spree at Ellerston. The property was developed into effectively a small kingdom, with several small homesteads in addition to the main, 13-bedroom house, along with a pub, restaurant, a general store, a cinema, a swimming pool, several man-made lakes and a school for employees' children.

Around 100 people live and work there, the majority of them looking after the various sporting and agricultural activities that comprised Packer's playground. Ellerston's polo facilities are said to be second to none in Australia.

Garry Linnell, former editor of *The Bulletin*, enjoyed the full Ellerston entertainment experience in 2003, on one of the executive retreats that Packer sometimes hosted there.

'They would fly you in and then bus you … We went into this amazing property. They had a big cinema, with black leather couches all tiered-up, and they'd often have Hollywood premiere movies up there, long before they got to the cinemas. Tennis courts, swimming pools, the Greg Norman-designed golf course …'

Packer, it seems, always had an outback-sized streak of the bush in him. The no-bullshit, foul-mouthed, often prickly personality that seemed so at odds with the billionaire businessman lifestyle, was absolutely at home in the hard-working environment of the Australian outback.

Out there, they'll respect the type of bloke who pulls a Brahman out of a dam—not the one who parks a Rolls-Royce in a swimming pool.

After Packer's suspected heart attack in 1983, the man he enlisted to start scouting for bush property was Ken Warriner.

The two men went back to the mid-1970s, when Warriner had been manager of Mount House Station in the Kimberley, in remote, far north-western Australia. Packer would trek up there to blow off some city steam.

'I was amazed 30 years ago at the hair-raising manner in which he would involve himself in catching wild bulls, chasing crocodiles, and donkey-shooting on foot,' Warriner told *The Bulletin* after Packer's death in 2005. 'KP was a very fit man.'

The outback provided Packer with an escape, not only in the physical environment, but perhaps also one of few where he could just be 'one of the boys'. And he took to it with typical Packer panache.

When Packer's bush push began in 1983, Warriner's suggestion had been to offer him Humbert River, a 1000 square kilometre station just south of Kakadu National Park, in the Northern Territory. It was one of two properties owned since 1979 by a partnership of experienced manager Warriner and prominent cattlemen Peter Baillieu and Tony Chisholm. Their other property was the much larger (10,500 square kilometres), but still somewhat run-down Newcastle Waters station, farther south.

Packer, in short order, convinced the trio to sell both properties. He installed Warriner as managing director with a 10 per cent holding in the company (Ashburton Pastoral Co) that would later become Consolidated Pastoral Company.

Packer's outback ambitions gained a huge nudge the following year, when he made a bid for the gem in Australia's northern cattle country, the 8900 square kilometre Victoria River Downs, which sits to the west of Newcastle Waters. A deal was contractually done, but at the 11th hour, the Northern Territory Government vetoed the sale.

Packer turned his attentions back to Newcastle Waters, and beyond. From his knowledge of the country, and from expert input from the likes of Warriner and fabled, fellow outback grazier and polo champion Sinclair Hill, Packer was developing a much broader vision for cattle farming.

'There's a club in Melbourne called the Savage Club. Lion's skins, it's very much a gentleman's club from 100 years ago, from the Boer War. Kerry would have been very much at home in that time.'

GARRY LINNELL, FORMER EDITOR, *THE BULLETIN*

'MANY PEOPLE, INCLUDING SOME OF THE DIEHARDS OF THE NORTH, HAVE SAID THAT THE BUSH IS A BETTER PLACE FOR KP'S INVOLVEMENT IN IT.'

Ken Warriner, Packer's bush buddy and managing director of Consolidated
Pastoral Company, quoted in *The Bulletin*, 4 January 2006

The previous partnership had bought Newcastle Waters in a run-down state, and was in the throes of building it up to compete with VRD. Packer effectively gave free rein to Warriner's management skills, backing him in a multi-million dollar spend on new fencing, equipment and dozens of new artesian bores (guess who named the Benaud and Bradman Bores?) Packer also built himself a grand, eight-bedroom homestead.

Warriner's signature strategy was to establish a network of top-class cattle breeding, holding and fattening facilities across the Top End, taking advantage of the best locations for each phase of the cattle production life cycle. Warriner restocked Newcastle Downs with Brahman heifers and breeders from Queensland, before buying a Brahman stud there. A similar Queensland stud was established for pure-bred Charolais bulls; these were crossed with pure-bred Brahmans to produce the hardy, yet high-quality hybrid Charbray.

On one exploratory tour of a potential property purchase, Packer and Warriner were lucky to not become mince-meat themselves, when both escaped the crash of a light aircraft. Details of the story are closely held, but it's believed that the two were aboard a station owner's Cessna, attempting to take off for an aerial tour of the property. The aircraft failed to clear a stand of trees at the end of the runway, tearing off a part of the wing and crashing to the ground.

Packer, although soaked in fuel, was mainly concerned with commandeering a nearby helicopter so as to complete the mission. Presumably, this was one time he didn't automatically reach for a cigarette ...

Strategic purchases like holding and fattening properties in Queensland's channel country and abattoirs in the Northern Territory built CPC into a monstrous, multi-national meat-making machine. The Australian station holdings of 5.8 million hectares in Queensland, the NT and Western Australia equated to 85 per cent of the land area of Tasmania.

'KP was particularly interested in breeding cattle that could handle the environment,' Warriner told *The Bulletin*.

'Everything had to be done to perfection. He was driven by the group's overall bottom line, rather than by quick profits. He invested in excess of $100 million in the pastoral industry at a time when far better investments were being put to him.

'But he loved the harshness and challenge of the north, and the sort of people who work this area. He had a great rapport with all and sundry—from truck drivers to head stockmen and meat workers—a genuine respect for them and those that pioneered this country before them.'

Warriner suggested that Packer's intervention and his drive for perfection may have been instrumental in the Australian cattle industry's survival on the international market. '[Packer] realised that improved processing was essential, not only for his own properties, but for a cattle industry generally that at the time was in dire straits. He genuinely wanted the whole industry to survive and prosper.'

Strangely, despite Packer's early enthusiasm for the outback and a continuing close eye on the CPC balance sheet, it's been reported that he ultimately stayed in his Newcastle Waters homestead on only a couple of occasions. According to Paul Myers in *The Australian* ('End of an era as Packer quits bush', 3 January 2009), his wife Ros Packer was a more regular visitor there.

Newcastle Waters is where Kerry dispatched his son James to serve a year of jackarooing, after he had completed high school. It was a case of history repeating: when Kerry's brother Clyde had asked his father about university, Sir Frank had replied, 'You go to work for me. You'll learn far more in the school of hard knocks.'

Kerry had had a similar response to the question of sending James to university. 'Why would he want to go there? To learn how to smoke marijuana?'

In 2009, James Packer shocked the rural world by selling his family's 90 per cent share of Consolidated Pastoral for $425 million to a British private equity firm. (Ken Warriner retained his 10 per cent). Two years later, a similar-sized sum relieved him of his 50 per cent share in the giant Teys Bros

cattle feed, processing and tannery business, another of his father's key acquisitions. But Ellerston Pastoral station is still owned and run by the Packer family.

Outback observers were sad to see the end of the Packer family's involvement in the cattle industry they had helped to revolutionise. At the same time, they were dipping their Akubras: in the timing, and the prices he got, James had done a deal worthy of his old man.

'You only get one Alan Bond in your lifetime, and I've had mine.'

Kerry Packer

4

THE DEALS

Kerry Packer was celebrated and slandered in equal measure for his ability to make boatloads of bucks. Whatever anyone said about the 'stupid son', the fact was that Packer parlayed a small fortune into Australia's largest—and by a long chalk.

In 1999, satirical group The Chaser thoughtfully introduced on its website, a Packer Watch Calculator. One of Australia's earliest such website devices, it enabled users to enter their annual salaries and see how long it would take Kerry Packer to earn it.

It was usually a matter of minutes. Journalist Alan Deans, writing in *The Bulletin*'s tribute issue to Packer on 4 January 2006, made a career calculation based on Packer's bookend entries in the *Business Review Weekly* magazine's annual Rich List. Packer was first listed in 1983, with a fortune of $100 million. His last entry in 2005, where he topped the list, was $6.9 billion.

That's $846,824 per day, for 22 years. And some believe that the *BRW* Rich List, diligently compiled by journalists using the best information they can access, gives the greatest satisfaction to tycoons in seeing how much of their wealth they've kept out of it. Again according to *BRW* in 2005, Packer ranked number 94 of the 691 billionaires in the world.

Channel Nine was the undisputed leader in television by any measure. ACP Magazines had an unmatched family of consistent money-earning titles, top among them the perennial *Australian Women's Weekly*. Along with all that came Consolidated Pastoral Company. Packer's purchase of Newcastle Waters and nearby Humbert River stations was the beginning of a 5 million hectare rural empire, one of Australia's largest and most innovative cattle exporters.

Inconveniently for Packer, his wealth didn't arrive in the form of $5.9 million weekly pay slips. It came through effectively just a handful of high-profile deals—most of them hits, but with a few notable misses—that spoke volumes for Packer's perception, persistence and flair for the art of doing business.

In 1983, Packer privatised Australian Consolidated Press in an audacious deal that, to begin with, exposed the little-known fact that the Packer family had actually owned only about one quarter of the shares in the company, this dating to a flurry of capital-raising in the dying days of Sir Frank. The rest was held by private and institutional investors.

KP's motive to privatise, it seems, wasn't purely Packer possessiveness. The timing was made perfect by a depressed share market and recent changes to the dividend-paying obligations of private companies.

Most pointedly, however, Packer sensed a change in the wind. The privatisation was part of a squirrelling strategy, in which he was locking down access to cash. On 17 December 1982, Packer told *The Australian Financial Review*: 'I have thought we were heading into a depression for the past 18 months to two years ... If the international banks do go broke and there's a depression, not a recession, those merchant banks out there might not have the money. They are in a far weaker situation than I am. So I can afford to have my money locked up, and can afford to pay the extra 0.5 per cent interest.'

Through a masterful structuring of shares and offers of tax-free dividends, and more than a little one-on-one Packer persuasion, the big fella privatised his media empire for around $100 million, or less than half the $220 million at which the assets had been valued.

But there were bigger deals to come. 'I want to live in

'I've read about Genghis Khan. He wasn't very lovable, but he was bloody efficient.'

KERRY PACKER

'Now, of course I am minimising my tax and if anybody in this country doesn't minimise their tax, they want their heads read. Because as a government, I can tell you that you're not spending it that well that we should be donating extra.'

Kerry Packer

'Kerry Packer revelled in his unpredictability, in his complexity, in his capriciousness. I was his lawyer and I said to him, "Kerry, this is a very bizarre way to run a public company" and he sat, he leant back in his chair, put his hands over his chest like that and he smiled and he said, "Ah, Malcolm, what you have overlooked is that I am a very bizarre person."'

Malcolm Turnbull, *Australian Story*, ABC TV, 7 April 2014

'Once the Bond team was in his office and a figure mentioned for the sale, Packer commenced to gaze moistly at his father's portrait.

"When I look at my father and wonder what he'd think of my selling Nine ... well, I don't think he'd want me to do it," sniffed the mogul. When the Bond team was gone—having agreed to a fabulous price—Packer spun to face Turnbull and winked.

"Now, son—how'd that go?" he asked.'

JOURNALIST ANNABEL CRABB RELATING A STORY TOLD BY MALCOLM TURNBULL, OF KERRY PACKER HASTILY HANGING A PORTRAIT OF SIR FRANK PACKER IN HIS OFFICE JUST PRIOR TO COMMENCING NEGOTIATIONS WITH ALAN BOND OVER THE SALE OF CHANNEL NINE. ANNABEL CRABB, *STOP AT NOTHING: THE LIFE AND ADVENTURES OF MALCOLM TURNBULL*

'He'd be doing mental arithmetic and I'd have to be doing the same thing. That's the way you had to be with him – if he asked you questions, you had to know with a certain amount of accuracy what could happen. Rupert Murdoch was exactly the same ... It was like playing squash with these guys, and the ball would keep coming from a different angle. It's not straightforward Yes and No stuff.'

Graham Lawrence

'I'm going to take three years off and get fit and then I'm going to come back and buy television stations for half the price their new owners just paid for them.'

KERRY PACKER TO JOHN D'ARCY OF THE *HERALD & WEEKLY TIMES*, AS REPORTED BY PAUL BARRY, *THE RISE AND RISE OF KERRY PACKER*

Australia,' Packer once said, 'but you have to protect your organisation by going overseas and by being defensive when investing in Australia.'

In 1986, he spent US$365 million on purchasing a US company, Valassis, which printed colour advertising inserts for newspapers and magazines. Valassis was by far the dominant player in the market.

The Valassis story is unusual in Packer's having remained fairly hands-off. He promoted an executive named David Brandon from within the Valassis ranks to CEO. Brandon helped increase sales by almost US$100 million in the first year, while also reducing the company's costs. In 1992, Packer decided to start cashing in on the hugely successful company, selling 51 per cent of his shares for US$375 million; in other words, pocketing US$10 million while retaining almost half of the company.

The remaining 49 per cent, sold in 1997, reaped a heady US$500 million. Through the machinations of corporate structure, dividends and so forth, however, many have estimated Packer's true Valassis harvest at somewhere between US$1–2 billion.

In the midst of that, in 1988 Packer spent a trifling $212 million to acquire most of the stable of magazines from familial rival Fairfax. These included the hugely successful *Woman's Day* and *People*, and perhaps ironically, *Cosmopolitan*; the magazine that had been the catalyst for Kerry's own initial magazine foray, *Cleo*. After the purchase, ACP held 50 per cent of the magazine market in Australia.

He also scored a significant win in acquiring 48 per cent of the distressed engineering conglomerate Australian National Industries in 1989. American corporate headkicker Al 'Chainsaw' Dunlap was installed and, when the sawdust settled just two and a half years later, Packer sold his share of ANI at a profit of $200 million.

He often seemed to have the punter's luck. Through 1987, Packer steadily built up a stake of around 12 per cent in the UK merchant bank, Hill Samuel. But by mid-year, he was becoming jittery about the world economy. Packer's lieutenant Trevor Kennedy went to London to offload the shares, eventually doing a deal that netted an $80 million profit.

That was in early October. Two weeks later, the share market crashed.

An even more audacious and slightly more profitable move on a bank occurred in 1992, when Packer acquired almost 10 per cent of Westpac for around $500 million. It was believed to be an advance action on a full-scale takeover, but Packer bailed out six months later—still bagging $100 million profit.

Author Paul Barry, in *The Rise and Rise of Kerry Packer*, reported that Packer's friendship with British financier Jimmy Goldsmith opened the door to a variety of international deals. In this rarefied atmosphere, it seemed, even to attempt takeovers and fail—as Goldsmith, Packer and co would do with Goodyear, British American Tobacco and others—would reap seven-figure profits.

Packer didn't always have the Midas touch or psychic signals. The debit side of his ledger included unsuccessful tilts on property deals, international takeovers, pay television investments, goldmines and a near-obsession with foreign exchange trading. The latter was said to have lost him half a billion dollars in 1993.

The biggest and best of Packer's deals was, of course, the selling of his beloved Nine Network to Alan Bond. It's the stuff of business legend that in January 1987, after the relaxation of national media ownership laws, acquisitive Perth signwriter Alan Bond came a-calling to revive an earlier discussion about selling his two Channel Nine stations in Perth and Brisbane.

Bond estimated his two stations were worth $400 million. Packer's eyebrows jumped. He mused on the likely value of *his* two Nines, in the far larger markets of Sydney and Melbourne.

Bond later claimed that Packer had thumped the table and declared them worth $1 billion, non-negotiable. But according to financial journalist Trevor Sykes, who has his say on the machinations of the deal in the excerpts below, it was Bond who ventured: 'Oh, they must be worth a billion dollars!'

'When they came out, he'd bought Packer's stations ... Bondy came out saying, "You should see the deal I've just done!" and his guys knew he'd got stung ... If Bondy didn't pay off the $200 million preference share in three years' time, Packer had the right to resume the stations—so he'd paid $800 million, *and he never had control*. Packer put all that stuff together.'

TREVOR SYKES

'Alan Bond, Frank Lowy and Christopher Skase all had monumental egos. Each of them wanted to be bigger, brighter, better, richer, more expansive, more extravagant than the other and none of them believed that making money was important.'

Kerry Packer to *The Bulletin* in December 1989, as he began circling the floundering Bond Media to eventually reclaim his beloved Nine

'There wouldn't be a businessman in Sydney—or in Australia, for that matter—who wouldn't accept my personal guarantee. I sold the *Telegraph* to Murdoch for sixteen million [*sic*] in the back of a car, and here I've got a snotty-nosed kid wanting my guarantee in writing for a lousy forty grand a year. You and your mate have got to be fucking kidding.'

KERRY PACKER TO TONY GREIG AND HIS MANAGER, BRUCE FRANCIS, DURING NEGOTIATIONS IN PARK ST FOR GREIG'S DEFECTION TO WORLD SERIES CRICKET. THE *TELEGRAPH* SUM WAS ACTUALLY $15 MILLION. AS TOLD IN *HOWZAT! KERRY PACKER'S WAR*

'I can't claim to have pinpointed the day of the crash. But it was obvious that something awful was going to happen. So, what was I to do? Sell. Get out.'

Kerry Packer, on the 1987 stock market crash

'I remember once, I was in his office, it was just me and him in there. The *Woman's Day* circulation was going up, he wanted to increase the advertising rates by about 50 per cent overnight. At the same time we're having this debate, he's on and off the phone to Jimmy Goldsmith every five minutes, doing this multi-billion dollar deal trying to take over British American Tobacco.

'I explained that I'd taken away the top discounts, the rates went up only three months ago ... This went on for about an hour. In the end he said, "Alright son, you've got me this time." And so I've been talking to Kerry Packer who's on the phone to Jimmy Goldsmith, taking over a billion-dollar company, and I went home late to my baked beans on toast.'

GRAHAM LAWRENCE

'Judged simply by financial criteria Kerry should have been proud of himself. And I remember he'd show me the graphs going up and up and up to Himalayan heights since he'd taken over. And he'd expect me and others to say "Gosh you're doing well Kerry, gosh you're doing well." He needed to hear it. He had to prove to the world and more importantly to himself that he was his father's son and that he was capable of building the business. And indeed he did.'

Phillip Adams, *Australian Story*, ABC TV, 7 April 2014

'Kerry once said to me, would I be a success if I wasn't a Packer? He'd say to me over and over again, could I have done it on my own? Could I have done it on my own?'

PHILLIP ADAMS, *AUSTRALIAN STORY*, ABC TV, 7 APRIL 2014

Packer knew only too well that his own advisers had valued his Sydney and Melbourne stations at $400 million.

With only Packer and Bond in the room—in Sydney's Intercontinental Hotel—one's thoughts drift to Packer's Park St office, and the painting of the lion and the gazelle, er, negotiating. Bond ended up paying $1.055 billion.

'Everyone thought [Packer] was wedded to TV forever,' says Sykes. 'But he'd made a billion dollars. I couldn't think of anything I wouldn't sell for a billion dollars ... And when you look at the way it was structured, Kerry always knew Bondy had just borrowed the stations.'

Packer, famously, made a photocopy of the cheque and had it hung on the back of the toilet door in his Park Street office.

Packer's foresight, or perhaps simply his reading of Bond's business abilities, left him in the front-row seat with $200 million worth of preference shares, to be paid off in three years' time. Should Bond be unable to pay them out, the show would be over and Packer would swoop back into control.

And so it came to pass.

Indeed, KP's impressive figure for selling a television network in Australia would—and perhaps could—only be surpassed by his son, James. In September 2007, less than two years after his father's death, James sold the Nine Network to venture capital firm CVC Partners for a total of $5.3 billion (comprising $1.9 billion in cash and $3.4 billion of debt).

Within a matter of weeks, the US would reel from the collapse of sub-prime mortgages and plunge most of the world into at least two years of financial crisis.

Kerry Packer was a dealer to the end. In mid-December 2005 he flew from Argentina, where he watched his Ellerstina team play in the Argentine Polo Open (the three-time champions lost, on this occasion), to formally bid $780 million for the rights to televise the Aussie Rules football from 2007–11. The offer was accepted on 23 December.

Within a fortnight, the rival consortium of Seven/Ten was forced to step up and beat Packer's bid. But by that time Packer, in the most final sense, had had the last word.

'Kerry and I started, in the Australian tradition, as enemies... He threatened to put me out of business because I kept bagging his *Australian Women's Weekly*. I (still) kept bagging it, so he did put me out of business. Then I threatened to put him out of business, but I was not sure how I would do it. So we met, I had 20 beers and he had 20 soft drinks and we became friends and I ended up doing all of Kerry's business, including the *Women's Weekly*.'

John Singleton, 'John Singleton, man of the people, always stays true to his words', Robert Craddock, *Courier-Mail*, 2 May 2013

THE NSW Supreme Court yesterday was told of a meeting where a critically ill Kerry Packer, heavily intubated in his hospital bed, trawled through details of One.Tel's cash flow with his son, One.Tel director James Packer, and other executives.

The meeting was in mid-February 2001 in Royal Prince Alfred Hospital in Camperdown, following Mr Packer's kidney transplant ...

Looking down at the spreadsheets, Kerry Packer then asked: 'What the f— is going on in June and July?'

FROM THE *SYDNEY MORNING HERALD*, 7 DECEMBER 2005, REPORTING ON THE ASIC'S ACTION AGAINST ONE.TEL FOR TRADING WHILE INSOLVENT IN 2001

'At one stage, he had [Sam] Chisholm and [Trevor] Kennedy in the room, they were talking about, you could do this and you do that ... and Kerry said, "As long as I've got a million a year to live on, I'll be happy, and you can have the rest." That was Kerry saying that. This was the earlier days—and of course, when he got richer and richer, that deal was forgotten!'

Graham Lawrence

5

PACKER UNDER FIRE

It became more than that for Kerry Packer when, in 1984, the Fairfax *National Times* newspaper published documents leaked from the royal commission, headed by Frank Costigan QC, on the notorious (and thankfully now defunct) Federated Ship Painters and Dockers Union.

The *National Times* story revealed the existence of a Mr Big, supposedly with interests in underworld activities.

Packer had given evidence the previous year about a cash loan, to do with a film-financing scheme, that linked him to some shady Queensland businessmen. Packer had received the $225,000 in cash, for reasons he explained bluntly: 'Because I like cash. I have a squirrel mentality. I like to keep cash. It is by no means the most cash I have ever had in my life.'

His codename in commission documents, Squirrel, was changed by the *National Times*, but Sydney was soon abuzz with gossip (even inner-city graffiti) that the 'Goanna' was Packer.

With legal lieutenant Malcolm Turnbull, Packer decided to go on the offensive. He identified himself as the central character and, in the 8000-word document that followed, proceeded to dismantle the allegations and innuendo that had arisen not so much from the commission, but the newspaper story.

Some of the allegations had bordered on comical. Then PM, Bob Hawke, described them as 'bullshit'. Packer was formally exonerated in 1987 by the Attorney-General, Lionel Bowen, but friends and family saw that it had been the most trying and damaging episode of his life.

Neither Packer, nor his family, would find it easy to forgive. At KP's memorial service 21 years after the episode, son James opined: 'It made [my father] a less trusting person, and I think it had an impact on his health.'

It may have been of some consolation to Packer that the National Times closed in 1987; part of a corporate malaise that, in turn, put Packer's ACP in the box seat to purchase Fairfax's magazine division the following year.

By 1990, while Packer was re-embracing Nine with his pockets full of Alan Bond's cash, John Fairfax Ltd was on its knees thanks to a brazen and bone-headed takeover attempt by 26-year-old family member, Warwick Fairfax.

The Fairfax empire of regional and major-city newspapers, including the flagship *Age* in Melbourne and the *Sydney Morning Herald*, was in the hands of receivers by December. The popular image was of Packer slavering to get at the wounded, graceful beast.

Under cross-media ownership laws that were in place at the time, however, Packer would have had to sell Nine, or be content with owning no more than 14.9 per cent of Fairfax. Having triumphantly reclaimed his beloved television stations less than six months earlier, selling Nine outright was highly unlikely. His quota of Alan Bond had been used.

Early in 1991, however, events conspired to put Packer together with Canadian media baron Conrad Black. The topic of Fairfax was evidently raised. Quite independently, frequent Packer associate Malcolm Turnbull was already circling Fairfax.

The consortium proposed by the three men, under the name Tourang, would divide the controlling share of Fairfax between Black, Packer and investment fund Hellman & Friedman—with Packer being strictly a non-executive director, with a 14.9 per cent holding.

The issue wasn't so much Packer, but Rupert Murdoch, who at that point controlled well over half the nation's newspaper circulation. With television-dominant Packer pitching a finger in the Fairfax pie, these two men would effectively exercise a duopoly on Australia's media. The cross-media ownership

'These innuendos and allegations arising from the inquiries of the royal commission have caused immense suffering on the part of my wife and children for nearly a year. They have been fuelled by what I believe has been vicious rumour and innuendo in newspapers controlled by commercial rivals of mine, John Fairfax & Sons ... Each and every one of the allegations made against me in the *National Times* article are [sic] false and demonstrably so ... so ludicrous and misconceived are the allegations, that my innocence is easily established.'

FROM KERRY PACKER'S PUBLIC STATEMENT, 28 SEPTEMBER 1984

'Most of them have never met me. There are the most enormous inaccuracies and perversions of the truth that I've ever read. I mean I read the stories about me and I don't like me.'

Kerry Packer replying to Jana Wendt's question about his reaction to newspaper criticism on *A Current Affair*, November 1991

'Mister Packer, could you please state your full name and the capacity in which you appear this afternoon, please?'

KP: 'Kerry Francis Bullmore Packer, I appear here this afternoon reluctantly.'

KERRY PACKER, WHILE APPEARING BEFORE THE HOUSE OF REPRESENTATIVES SELECT COMMITTEE ON PRINT MEDIA ON 4 NOVEMBER 1991

'I'm never happy to answer questions but that's never stopped anyone putting them to me.'

Kerry Packer door-stopped by reporters

'I KNOW WHO I AM, MY FRIENDS KNOW WHO I AM AND THE REST CAN GET FUCKED.'

Kerry Packer to Alan Jones, *The Bulletin*, 4 January 2006

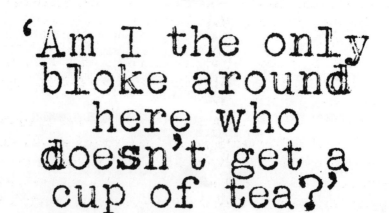

'Am I the only bloke around here who doesn't get a cup of tea?'

Kerry Packer, while appearing before the House of Representatives Select
Committee on Print Media on 4 November 1991

rules had been implemented to avoid precisely this situation.

Fuelled largely by the Fairfax papers themselves, opposition to any further Packer play mounted quickly. It even included the entirely unexpected combination of former prime ministers Gough Whitlam and Malcolm Fraser, who both signed a protest letter circulated by senior politicians. The Hawke government announced small, but significant changes and tighter policing of the cross-media ownership rules.

For the Tourang bid to succeed, Packer had to paint himself as a silent and disinterested investor. Not for the first time, he provided an interview to *A Current Affair*, which he used for his public relations pitch. 'For 50 years of my life, Fairfax has been competition to me and my family,' he told Jana Wendt. 'The idea that I can end up buying 15 per cent...amuses me.'

Subsequent events would prove that Packer was being downright dishonest about his ambitions with Fairfax. The Tourang bid would eventually be withdrawn, apparently upon discovery that one of the insiders in the deal had handed over documents that proved Packer's inevitable and innate urge to seize executive power despite his limited shareholding.

But three weeks before the bid was abandoned, it produced one of Packer's most memorable public performances, before the House of Representatives Select Committee on Print Media on 4 November 1991.

Packer was in understandably combative mood from the off. The ABC TV's camera crews jostled to position and ready themselves; Packer's appearance in front of the committee, unusually, was being televised live. Packer shuffled some papers and harrumphed at the committee chairman, 'It'd be nice if we got all the photographs done, then we can get down to action being serious about it, rather than just being a circus.'

What followed was 116 minutes of Kerry Francis Bullmore Packer at his charming, bullying, witty and withering best. Openly declaring the whole exercise 'an intellectual wank', he proceeded to make mincemeat of politicians (and politics), through astute observations that resonated at every level from the very Constitution of Australia, to the man in the street.

KP: 'Constitutionally, there's got to be an enormous argument that you have no right to enquire into print media, at all ...'

[later] John Langmore: 'Are you saying, Mister Packer, that you don't think Parliament has the right to enquire into the print media?'

KP: 'Yes, I am saying exactly that ...'

Q: 'So you don't think Parliament has the responsibility ...'

KP: 'I don't think under the Constitution you have the right to do it.'

Q: 'Can I finish my question. The national parliament has the responsibility for looking at any aspect of public policy which it judges to be appropriate.'

KP: 'You, you seem to be completely unaware of the Constitution of Australia, which you as a politician have to abide by, the same as everybody else. My view is that under the Constitution, you don't have the right.'

Q: 'But the lawyers ...'

KP: 'The lawyers also hold that view, almost equally. Whether you do or whether you don't. Now if you really want to, you can go to the High Court and find out.'

Q: 'No lawyer that's come before us has questioned that we have the right to do that.'

KP: 'Maybe you haven't asked them the question.'

KERRY PACKER, WHILE APPEARING BEFORE THE HOUSE OF REPRESENTATIVES SELECT COMMITTEE ON PRINT MEDIA ON 4 NOVEMBER 1991

KP: 'I thought that was a privileged document ...'

Jeannette McHugh, Labor: 'I've just given you an example, Mr Packer ...'

KP: 'You've given me an example of what?'

Q: 'Of how, if people need to get around ...'

KP: 'You've given me an example of something that I was exonerated from and hijacked into before—the Costigan inquiry—and you're sitting here under parliamentary privilege dragging that up again. I think you've got a damned hide.'

KERRY PACKER, WHILE APPEARING BEFORE THE HOUSE OF REPRESENTATIVES SELECT COMMITTEE ON PRINT MEDIA ON 4 NOVEMBER 1991

'The laws get twisted and changed, the whole structure gets moved around, depending on whether they like the colour of your eyes or not. Now, if we were a little bit more worried about jobs out there and getting people to invest money in this country and getting some businesses going, instead of trying to stop people ...'

Kerry Packer

'Why do you want to change the rules again? I mean, since I grew up as a boy, I would imagine that, through the Parliaments of Australia, from the time I was 18, 19 years of age to now, there must be 10,000 new laws been passed. And I don't really think it's that much better a place. And I'd like to make a suggestion to you, which I think would be far more useful. If you want to pass a new law, why don't you only do it when you've repealed an old one? I mean, this idea of just passing legislation, legislation every time someone blinks, is a nonsense. Nobody knows it, nobody understands it, you've got to be a lawyer, got books up to here—purely and simply to do the things we used to do. And every time you pass a law, you take somebody's privileges away from them.'

KERRY PACKER

Q: 'If you exercise the rights for the pre-emptive purchase of the junk bond holders, what effect does that have on the shareholding structure of Tourang, as we now know it from the information given by Mr [Trevor] Kennedy?'

KP: 'None at all. None at all. Tourang will be out of the business by then. But, if you think I'm going to be railroaded and sit here and be told that you're going to change the laws and you're going to push me around, I may well buy them.'

Kerry Packer, while appearing before the House of Representatives Select
Committee on Print Media on 4 November 1991

'He doesn't *have* to do anything, and I don't have to do anything. You can't tell us what we have to do. He's a private company. He's a private citizen. He's not an elected politician. He's not a public company. I'm not a politician. I don't have to answer questions from journalists. We don't *have* to do anything.'

PACKER'S REPORTED RESPONSE TO JOURNALIST DAVID DALE, EDITOR OF *THE BULLETIN* FROM
1988–91, WHEN DALE BEGAN TO OUTLINE THE RULES FOR AN INTERVIEW WITH PROPERTY
DEVELOPER AND PACKER PAL, WARREN ANDERSON. *FOUR CORNERS*, ABC TV, 16 SEPTEMBER 1991

John Langmore: 'What the [ABC TV] *Four Corners* program suggested was not that you were evading tax at all, that would have been libellous, but that you were minimising tax ...'

KP: 'There's nothing wrong with minimising tax—I don't know anybody who doesn't minimise their tax.'

Q: '... and that you were doing so in ways that were contrary to the spirit of the law.'

KP: 'Uggh. Well, I just got through telling you what I thought about that. And what you're saying is exactly what the *Four Corners* program says. I am not evading tax in any way, shape or form.'

Kerry Packer, while appearing before the House of Representatives Select Committee on Print Media on 4 November 1991

'The "Goanna" material goes on to suggest that I have a lavish and expensive lifestyle and that my considerable assets are insufficient to provide the cash resources necessary to support both my lavish livings and my gambling. As anyone who knows me would attest, both my lifestyle and my gambling are well within my means ...'

from Kerry Packer's public statement, 28 September 1984

Part 2

PACKER AT PLAY

'In many ways, he was acting out the fantasies of millions of Australian punters. They weren't the only ones awestruck by the size of the bets. So were we.'

James Packer at Kerry Packer's State memorial service, Sydney Opera House, 17 February 2006

'WE HAVE A SLANG TERM FOR BIG TIPPERS ... IT'S CALLED GEORGE. AND KERRY PACKER'S A SUPER GEORGE ...'

Steve Cyr, Las Vegas casino host, interviewed on ABC Radio by Rafael Epstein, 30 September 2004

6

TOSS YOU FOR IT

'Investing' a six- or seven-figure sum in a game of baccarat or on the spin of a roulette wheel would seem anathema to Kerry Packer's personality. Some may attempt to explain it as a big man who, accustomed to operating on a big scale, needed super-sized thrills.

The Big Man himself once conceded: 'Betting is like a disease, which is not understood by those who do not have it.'

Packer once took Garry Linnell of *The Bulletin* on a verbal tour of Sydney's mean streets of the 1950s and 60s. The young KP may have been the scion of a media dynasty, but in the early days he was paid miserably by his father—who, it was said, took much of it back again in board. Packer well knew these inner-Sydney alleys of illegal casinos, sly grog shops and SP (starting-price) bookmakers.

'He inhabited that town when Sydney wasn't all sparkling like it is today,' Linnell says. 'Sydney was a tough town, it was run largely by gangsters, through all these backstreet meetings and dens of iniquity. Kerry moved within it, and then he moved above it. Kerry's greatest passion was gambling. He lost and won big money.'

From those shifty wagers with backstreet bookies and illegal casinos, Packer's gambling career would blossom well beyond Australia. Among the *casinoscenti* of Las Vegas, London and elsewhere, for more than two decades Packer ranked with the Sultan of Brunei and arms dealer Adnan Kashoggi as a prince of the 'whales'—ultra-high net worth, international gamblers who regularly won and lost in seven figures.

The scraps left in the wake of such frenzies were neither to be scoffed at. Packer's tipping of casino staff became so well-known that, as one insider put it, 'There was no-one sicker than a croupier genuinely taken sick when Packer was in town.'

In the *Las Vegas Review Journal* in 2005 Mirage Resorts president Bobby Baldwin confirmed a well-known story, about an extremely generous tip given to a lucky cocktail waitress at the MGM Grand. 'He liked the service the girl was providing. He asked her if she had a mortgage. She said yes, and he said, "Bring it in tomorrow and I'll pay it off for you". It was for US$150,000.'

A similar story told in *Whale Hunting in the Desert: Secrets of a Las Vegas Superhost* has Packer accidentally bumping a cocktail waitress, causing her to spill her drinks tray. Packer asked for her name and address and saw to it that her US$130,000 mortgage was immediately mopped up.

And it seems Kerry Packer was as determined in his generosity as he was in everything else. Garry Linnell reported yet another mortgage-magic act in Vegas, where Packer pushed US$80,000 worth of chips towards a deserving croupier. The croupier blushed and explained that she couldn't accept it; all tips had to be pooled and shared among the staff.

Packer called the manager and insisted that he fire her on the spot, on the threat of taking his business elsewhere. When the manager complied, Packer handed her the chips. He then turned to the manager: 'Now rehire this woman immediately.'

The most celebrated story has Kerry Packer playing cards at a table in the Bellagio, which opened in 1998 as the flagship property of casino king Steve Wynn's Mirage Resorts group. Mirage Resorts boss Bobby Baldwin confirmed the story to casino roundsman Norm Clarke in the *Las Vegas Review-Journal* in the days after Packer's death.

Packer was playing at one table and a loud-mouthed Texan, playing at the next table, wanted to join in. He didn't take too kindly to the Australian's rejection.

Barry Humphries ... after hearing of fellow Aussie/high roller Kerry Packer's death, 'I looked out my window expecting to see the casinos covered in black crepe.' The whale of whales, Packer, 68, died on Monday.

Las Vegas Review Journal, 28 December 2005

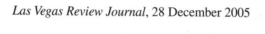

'He went over to London and I think he went to the Ritz Casino. There were reports in the paper that he'd lost $22 million in a weekend and it was a very big deal in Australia at the time. I said, this looks bad, this looks terrible. He said, "You don't understand gambling, do you?" And I said, no, you explain it to me. And he said, "If you really are a gambler, the only thing that matters is it has to hurt if you lose. And I've got to lose a lot of fucking money before it hurts."'

Labor politician Graham Richardson (once nicknamed the Minister for Kerry Packer), *Australian Story*, ABC TV, 14 April 2014

'Son, never worry about the money, always worry about winning first.'

Kerry Packer giving Kiwi trainer John Bary a lesson on gambling. "Packer taught Kiwi trainer a lesson", Ray Thomas, *The Daily Telegraph*, 24 March 2011

According to Baldwin: 'The [Texan] said, "I'm a big player too. I'm worth $100 million". Kerry said, "If you really want to gamble, I'll flip you for it" … The Texan quietly went back to his game.'

In Texas parlance, they call that "all hat and no cattle".

Gambling was play for Kerry Packer, so the normal rules of business evidently did not apply. The scale and rate at which he operated made him difficult to keep up with. Neither Packer nor his people maintained P&L statements on his multimillion-dollar binges, and if the casinos did—those that could handle him, anyway—they weren't saying.

Most of the Big Fella's best casino splurges occurred overseas. In Las Vegas, where the touchdown of KP's converted DC-8 three or four times a year would instantly set the jungle drums a-humming, Packer was known as a 'hit and run' player. He would turn up at any hour of the day or night and bet big, often with several hands of blackjack going at once. If the winning was good, after a couple of hours he might disappear into the night.

Casinos consider that poor etiquette. Still, they lured Packer and his fellow whales by reimbursing their travel expenses (said to be up to $100,000 for Packer and his entourage) and offering 'rebates' on their losses. Frank 'Lefty' Rosenthal, on whom Robert DeNiro's character in *Casino* was based, confirmed to *The Australian* newspaper in August, 2000 that Packer received a 10 per cent rebate.

The Vegas trips were usually short and sharp: three or four days of hitting the big-dollar blackjack and baccarat tables along the Strip. According to casino host Steve Cyr, subject of the book *Whale Hunt in the Desert*, Packer was 'a pretty good blackjack player' who had had some tutoring. Less courageous casinos became wary of booking his blackjack bets.

Cyr said this was in part because Packer was known to be more placid when playing baccarat. 'He didn't go off on temper tantrums as much at baccarat … Because decision-making comes into play at the blackjack table, he was a lot more volatile when playing 21.'

In London, Packer seemed to be in less of a hurry, sometimes idly spreading a splurge over a few days. But the size of the wins and losses were no less impressive. Indeed, Packer supposedly claimed a variety of dubious honours—the first eight-figure loss in one sitting, the biggest loss in British casino history, and being barred from or even bankrupting casinos by winning too much—pretty well equally across both continents.

Apparently celebrating his sale of Nine to Alan Bond, Packer had a flutter at the private blackjack tables at London's Ritz. Reportedly played two tables at £10,000 per hand, he could have bought a lot of cake and candles with the £8 million dump he took.

London was the scene of another landmark a little over a year later. The London casino Aspinall's went broke in May 1990, and London's *Today* newspaper blamed Packer.

November 1991 had Packer in Las Vegas, scooping $7 million on blackjack. Gossip columnist Nigel Dempster reported him handing out $50,000 tips to the croupiers on that occasion. But in the same year—possibly the same visit—Vegas casino host Steve Cyr reported Packer copping a $10 million hit at the Las Vegas Hilton. It was the biggest single-session loss in the hotel's history.

It's not a feat you'd be keen to repeat, but Packer supposedly lost a further $10 million to the same hotel in 1992. By which time, thanks to his previous loss, they'd been prompted to upgrade their cage computer to accept eight-figure hauls.

These must have been extraordinary stand-offs: Packer and the casinos both knew that he could, single-handedly, either bankrupt or buy them.

As it was, Packer's plays were significant enough that a casino company's earnings could be clobbered, and its market capitalisation nudged by whole percentage points. And it could swing either way in the course of one sitting. Deke Castleman, in *Whale Hunt in the Desert*, reports Packer

A story has long gone around Las Vegas that in the late '80s, Packer had a $5 million credit line at Caesars. It was as large a line as anyone could get at the time, but he still wanted to increase his credit. He got on the phone with the president of Caesars and said, "Look, I can buy this company with petty cash."

The president said, "Great. When you buy the company, you can give yourself any credit line you want. But while we still own it, you'll have to abide by our limits."

Deke Castleman, *Whale Hunt in the Desert*

'One of the greatest moments of his life was, we went into Crockford's one night, in London, and the manager came out and greeted Kerry and took him aside—he wanted to have a private conversation with him. And Kerry came back with a big grin, ear to ear, all over his face. And he said "Well, one thing that I've always wanted to happen to me," he said, "I've been banned from a casino for winning too much!" And Crockford's actually banned him because he had taken, I dunno, about 10 million quid off them in the previous couple of weeks. And they'd had enough.'

PACKER LIEUTENANT AND SOMETIME GAMBLING PAL TREVOR KENNEDY, INTERVIEWED ON *THE EXTRAORDINARY LIFE OF KERRY PACKER*, CHANNEL NINE, 16 FEBRUARY 2006

'He regularly tipped Bellagio dealers US$1 million, all 700 dealers would get a cut'

Mirage Resorts president Bobby Baldwin to the
Las Vegas Review Journal in 2005

'What most neglect to mention is how angry Packer sometimes made those casino executives feel when he'd hit it big at the tables, then pass out a fortune to the dealers. Word is there was even talk of asking him not to be quite so generous with the hired help. But Packer's will prevailed, as it almost always did.'

'Packer's Green', *Las Vegas Review Journal*, 30 December 2005

'I did a sales trip to London around the mid-1980s. I knew he always stayed at the Savoy, so I thought if I booked myself in there, I might get something decent. I'd been in the hotel for five minutes and the phone rang, it was Pat Wheatley. She said, "Now you've arrived, you'd better go and see the old man." So I went up to see him and he was sitting in a dressing gown. He'd just had the kidney out. He said, "How are you, son?" I asked how *he* was feeling, he said "Oh, a bit worn-out." I was feeling very sorry for him, he was looking very tired and weak. When I phoned Trevor Kennedy, I told him [Packer] wasn't looking very good. Kennedy said, "No wonder he wasn't looking too good. He'd been down at the casino till four o'clock in the morning."'

GRAHAM LAWRENCE, FORMER ACP ADVERTISING EXECUTIVE

'Kerry was a friend, a great friend, but at the same time it's often quite difficult to negotiate with friends. I needed $180,000 and Kerry was not going to go beyond $150,000 ... So I said, "Why don't we toss for it?" And he said, "OK. You call." I said, "Tails." He at the other end, I couldn't see him do it, but I knew he was tossing the coin. And he said, "Frosty old son, you win."'

Sir David Frost, describing the phone call that landed his career-boosting, $2 million interview with disgraced US President, Richard Nixon. *Sunday Night*, Channel Seven, 30 September 2012

walking into Caesars Palace on the night of 31 March, 1992 and being $9 million ahead of the house by midnight. At that hour Caesars closed the book on its financial quarter, and what was petty cash to Packer was a 50 per cent hit to the casino's first-quarter profits. By dawn, however, 'Packer lost back the $9 million and then some'.

Back in London, in 1994, the new owners of Crockford's received a windfall on their second day when KP dropped the equivalent of US$7 million. But far bigger adventures awaited back in Vegas the following year, when Packer had the dual satisfactions of belting the MGM Grand for six and being banned for life.

Reports of the wee-hours winning blitz, and the sums involved, have Packer simultaneously playing six hands at $75,000 per hand, or eight hands at $250,000. *Whale Hunt in the Desert* author Castleman has Packer eventually being allowed to play $500,000 a hand—and walking off in just a couple of hours with a $26 million haul.

Packer liked the feel of it, and returned for several more visits. But MGM International Resorts supremo Kirk Kerkorian, who'd got to know Packer over several dinners, put his foot down: Packer was banned from MGM's casinos.

Castleman's book reports that one of Kerkorian's executives—a dedicated MGM 'Packer handler'—was flown to England to break the news to Packer, who was playing polo. Packer sent his helicopter to bring the guy from Heathrow to his Fyning Hill estate. The executive came back to report that Packer had threatened to make him walk back to London; but that he had sensed in Packer a strange sort of satisfaction on Packer's part.

Tales of Packer's punting exploits in Australia and South-East Asia are few, but Nigel Dempster reported Packer swooping on Jupiter's on the Queensland Gold Coast in 1998, distributing $300,000 in tips to four hostesses after an unspecified 'lucky run'. There again, he was known to distribute similar-sized tips after a loss.

Packer may or may not have been in a generous mood when,

in September 1999, a £11 million hit at Crockford's blackjack tables over a three-week period supposedly set a new record for the biggest loss in UK casino history. (One suspects he was beating his own record, set at the Ritz a dozen years earlier.)

It may be significant that 1999 was also the year in which Packer effectively took out some gambling insurance, taking over Melbourne's Crown Casino complex from his punting mate, Lloyd Williams. Packer later added Perth's Burswood Casino (2004) and introduced to Australia the online betting exchange, Betfair (2005).

Meanwhile, in July 2000 Packer was again in Las Vegas, but luck—and his desire to fly under the radar—firmly deserted him. No longer welcome at the MGM Grand, he turned his attention to the lavish new Bellagio, which casino king Steve Wynn had opened 18 months earlier.

In three days at the baccarat tables, Packer managed to scorch through US$20 million, a sum that may have extended his record-holding status across the Atlantic.

But the story would go farther than that. Such was the mystique surrounding Kerry Packer that, when a small news item in a Las Vegas paper was picked up by *The Australian* newspaper on 30 August, more than a month later, all hell broke loose.

The newspaper's LA correspondent Robert Lusetich wrote of Packer's US$20 million hit, equating to A$34 million, and linked it with the London loss 10 months earlier.

On 31 August, erratic Labor politician Mark Latham stood up in the House of Representatives and opened a speech with the words: 'I wish to reflect on the news that Australia's richest man, Kerry Packer, lost $34 million last month on a gambling spree in Las Vegas. I am sure that most Australians will feel uneasy about this sort of extravagance. Notions of public morality and justice are under threat when it is possible for one person to accumulate such extraordinary wealth and then use it in such an extraordinary way.'

Latham went on to add: 'Surely those who have been fortunate enough to accumulate considerable wealth should

One night, in the fall of 1989, after Packer blew into Las Vegas and found his way to the newly opened Mirage, the baccarat crew was not quite ready for him. A graveyard-shift pit boss couldn't find the key to unlock the game at a table that had been reserved for Australia's most notorious billionaire. There was only one sensible option: grab a crystal ashtray, smash open the baccarat setup and begin dealing. Famously sporty Packer appreciated the effort. After getting ahead a couple million dollars, he made a $100,000 bet on behalf of the dealers.

Michael Kaplan, 'Remembering the World's Greatest Gambler',
Cigar Aficionado, Mar-Apr 2006

In 1991, [casino host] Steve Cyr saw Jimmy Newman, the senior vice-president of Hilton Corporation, and Guy Hudson, the senior vice-president of Hilton credit, *running* across the casino. These guys were casino *gods*; they were *never* in a hurry. And here they were at full sprint all the way from the front to the back of the joint, looking like they were being chased by demons.

It turned out that early the night before, Kerry Packer had shown up unexpectedly at the Hilton's high-limit pit, but it was closed and wouldn't open for an hour. Packer walked right back out the door and heads rolled. The next night, Packer pulled up again unannounced; warned by the valet manager, Newman and Hudson were in a rush to make sure the room was ready for him.

He lost $10 million that night. It was a record at the time— the first time anyone had lost eight figures in one session. Hilton bean counters couldn't get the size of the loss into the computer, which only accepted up to seven digits.

DEKE CASTLEMAN, *WHALE HUNT IN THE DESERT*

use it in a socially responsible fashion. Blowing $34 million at a casino is not a very responsible thing to do.'

Packer fired back in the following day's edition of *The Australian*, asserting that it was his money and, rare for him, revealing that he had only recently given a larger sum than that to a Sydney children's hospital.

Prime Minister John Howard, who was certainly on friendlier terms with Packer than he was with Latham, surprisingly also stepped forward in his defence: 'I thought the Latham attack was ludicrous ... It is his money. He made the very legitimate point that he doesn't gamble with his company's money, and if you look at his corporate record that is right.'

Lost on Latham, of course, was the obvious fact that Packer's $34 million was not actually 'blown' at all. Like water, or energy, it had merely changed form, in this case being redistributed to the casino, its employees, and to the people of Nevada via the state's tax income.

The Kerry kerfuffle of September 2000 inevitably calmed down, but Packer wasn't happy. A year later, in early September 2001, Packer returned to the Bellagio and demanded that his hotel minders sign confidentiality agreements. And the dealers got some inkling of his anger when he refused to tip them.

He then proceeded to lose even more. According to Norm Clarke of the *Las Vegas Review Journal* Packer was playing baccarat at up to $150,000 a hand, and occasionally took breaks to play blackjack and munch hot dogs at the sports book. Packer ended up losing a staggering US$29 million, or close to $50 million in Oz currency.

He wasn't even meant to still be in Vegas. But the events of 11 September 2001, which grounded his plane for at least a week beyond his planned departure date, put the frivolous fortunes of a card game sharply into perspective.

'If Kerry won, he would always give you a share of his winnings. I remember once in London he tossed me a packet of notes—it was about £10,000. He was a generous man.'

Tony Greig, cricketer and close friend, who regularly accompanied Packer on international casino trips. *The Bulletin*, 4 January 2006

'I've personally watched the man wager $200,000 for the dealers on one hand. And they won, several times!'

LAS VEGAS DEALER IN AN EMAIL TO NORM CLARKE, CA.1999, CITED IN *LAS VEGAS REVIEW JOURNAL*, 28 DECEMBER 2005

'After noticing that a blackjack dealer had been moved from the high-limit area to the regular pit, he placed £15,000 bets on each spot and told the dealer that he could keep all winnings from that round.'

'Gamblers: Kerry Packer', bet-like-a-pro.com

The story goes that Packer was flying somewhere—Singapore, Bangkok, London—from Sydney and he called the cage at the Darwin Casino at the northern tip of Australia, which was on his flight path. He asked the cage supervisor how much cash was on hand. When he was given a number, he said no thanks. When the supervisor asked him how much cash he needed to stop off and play, he quoted three times the number.

The next time Packer called, Darwin had enough cash in the cage and he landed. He played, won and emptied the cage. He tipped everyone well and took off again, with a little extra walking-around money for his trip.

DEKE CASTLEMAN, *WHALE HUNT IN THE DESERT*

Friends say he has a photographic memory and the ability to calculate instantly the odds on what card the dealer will turn over next. At Crockford's, where Mr Packer gambles when he is in London, the maximum bet on any hand of blackjack is £250,000. He will often bet this on all seven hands dealt to the table.

Mr Packer is known for his gentlemanly conduct in casinos. A friend said: 'I once saw him lend the actor George Hamilton £125,000 in chips. Hamilton had two aces and wanted to split them but didn't have enough money. Hamilton hit 21 with both aces but Kerry refused to accept anything other than his loan back.'

'GAMBLER PACKER LOSES £13 MILLION IN 3 DAYS', SIMON DAVIS, *THE TELEGRAPH* (UK),
31 AUGUST 2000

'Some of the happiest times I ever saw my dad was times when I was with him in the casinos and he had a good night.'

James Packer, interviewed in *Forbes magazine*, March 2014

'When politicians start becoming moral judges on what people can spend their money on or not is, I think, something which sits better in a Stalinist state than in this country ... My motto basically is: never complain, never explain. I take risks which are for my own recreation, which sometimes work out and sometimes don't. I can assure you, it's less money than I gave to the Children's Hospital in Westmead, Sydney.'

Kerry Packer to *The Australian*, 1 September 2000, in response to Mark Latham's criticism of his reported $34 million loss in Las Vegas

'Son, don't worry about how big the bet was. Remember one thing: the biggest bet you can have is the one you can't afford to pay.'

JAMES PACKER QUOTING HIS FATHER, AT KERRY PACKER'S STATE MEMORIAL SERVICE, SYDNEY OPERA HOUSE, 17 FEBRUARY 2006

'Afterwards, he took a few of us out to Aspinall's ... Kerry gave us some chips to gamble with after dinner. It wasn't a ridiculous amount, maybe £100—but in the process, he lost a few hundred *thousand* pounds at the tables. The thing that amused me somewhat was that he paid for his debt with his American Express card!

'A few weeks later, back at The Dorchester [Packer's hotel], I remember Pat Wheatley ringing from Sydney ... Pat's ringing to say that she's got this bill from American Express which she'd rejected—it was for a few hundred thousand pounds, and she's obviously said to them, "No, you've made a mistake, go back and check your figures". What I remember is Kerry, at the end of the conversation: "Pat, just effin' pay it."

'His demeanour didn't change at all. It was basically, "Well, you win some, you lose some..."'

GREG CHAPPELL, ON HIS FIRST MEETING WITH KERRY PACKER IN LONDON, 1977

'He was one of the first customers I ever watched bet over $100,000 a hand. And I can remember many a night watching him bet $75k, $100k, $150k a hand ... He was a very disciplined player. He'd hit and run. He hurt a lot of casinos with that. Hit and run means you only come in, play a couple of shoes, win a million bucks, and walk right out the door ... He wasn't there to get plastered and have a good time—he was there to win ... one year ... I was in the top bonus pool, and when we hit a certain percentage above our EBIT at which is, you know, New Year's Eve, we were right there, we were supposed to make, like $54 million or something like that—and we were over it, we were at like $61 million, and I was to get a six-figure bonus. Kerry Packer came in and won $13 million on New Year's Eve and crushed us, and I got nothing.'

STEVE CYR, CASINO HOST INTERVIEWED ON ABC RADIO BY RAFAEL EPSTEIN, 30 SEPTEMBER 2004

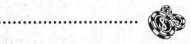

After the Crockford's losses, a friend was quoted as saying: 'Kerry probably will not mind too much. It is probably the casino's money anyway.'

'Packer loses $20 million at cards', BBC News, 31 August 2000

'He's not afraid to win. You know what I mean? Like, he'll bet the max, win a couple million, and then the bad news is he might take it to another casino and lose it ... and that's the worst thing that can happen in our job. When I was at the Hilton one night, he won $3 million and took it to Caesar's Palace. I mean, then you want to throw up in a trash can, you know what I mean?'

Steve Cyr, casino host interviewed on ABC Radio by Rafael Epstein,
30 September 2004

More recently [ca.2001–05], following a particularly brutal cash-grabbing rage through Vegas—which, according to Cyr, 'ended with [Packer] winning $20 million at four joints and $13 million at another one'— several casino bosses tried to minimise the danger of going up against an inveterate gambler who seemed to have bottomless resources, no qualms about dropping millions of dollars, and an understanding of variance swings. 'Everyone finally said, "To hell with this guy,"' recalls Cyr. 'And they decided to keep him at 25 grand per bet.'

MICHAEL KAPLAN, 'REMEMBERING THE WORLD'S GREATEST GAMBLER', *CIGAR AFICIONADO*, MAR-APR 2006

'You know, the only negative about Mr P is that he lives in Australia, so when are you going to get him at the most ... three times a year? Okay, and that's at the most. I'd rather have a guy that's half a million dollar line, but lives in southern California, but he's coming up every couple of weeks.'

Steve Cyr, Las Vegas casino host, interviewed on ABC Radio by Rafael Epstein, 30 September 2004

'His real gambling was on foreign exchange. Some nights he came close to betting the farm on the US dollar against the Deutschmark. James was quite petrified by it. We're talking late 1980s. He would take very big positions in the overnight market ... By Christ, he was really putting his shirt on it sometimes. Packer was just gambling, and it was really rather frightening. I heard one or two numbers on it and they were so large, it took my breath away.'

Trevor Sykes, former editor, *The Bulletin*

'IT TURNED OUT SHITHOUSE, DIDN'T IT?'

Kerry Packer to Ken Callander, after finishing
$960,000 down on a day's punting in January
1984. *Good Luck and Good Punting*

7

THE TURF

According to his daughter Gretel, Kerry Packer was 'a complete softie when it came to horses.' Packer had an intuitive understanding of the beasts, even if ideas on equine nutrition may have been influenced by his own: when KP was at Ellerston, the finely-tuned, four-legged athletes would feast on packets of Nice biscuits.

The passion for ponies naturally included the punt. Between casino blitzes in Las Vegas and London, the turf provided Packer with instant gambling gratification to stave off his bouts of boredom.

He kept a large stable of polo ponies—and a stable of *large* polo ponies—but he also owned or co-owned several top-flight racehorses over the years. That's despite what his footy mate, legendary South Sydney supremo George Piggins recalled Packer once telling him over a quiet dinner: 'Anyone owning a football team or a racehorse is mad.'

Packer, of course, owned both (he financially backed the East Sydney rugby league club), but as Piggins explained years later, 'Kerry was interested in sport and he put his money where his mouth was.'

One of the great racehorses of the mid-1990s was Mahogany. Packer jointly owned the thoroughbred with his great punting mate, property developer Lloyd Williams. Fathered in 1990 by a stallion named (appropriately) Last Tycoon, Mahogany racked up at least eight major victories and around $3.7 million in prize money.

Sounds like a good investment. But Packer had offered some proof of the profligacy of thoroughbred ownership in a conversation with writer Les Carlyon, who quoted Packer in *The Bulletin*.

'Now you take my best year—the year when Mahogany won all those derbies and was made horse of the year and all that,' Packer said, referring to the 1993-94 season. 'You'd reckon if you had a horse as good as him you'd be a mile in front, wouldn't you? Well, when I totted up the running costs on the rest of my racehorses, I was out two million bucks for the year.'

Carlyon reported that Packer, in telling the story, burst out laughing.

But it was Packer's huge, sporadic spends from outside the rails that equally caught the attention of the turf fraternity. In the betting rings at Australia's racecourses, where his wagers reached Vegaspheric heights during the 1980s-90s, the bookies knew him as 'Buckets'.

As always, Packer knew what he was doing, and he was doing it to win. Since the 1970s, he'd cultivated friendships with jockeys. He got his race tips almost from the horse's mouth. Jockey Greg 'The G' Hall, who often rode for Packer and Williams, told Patrick Carlyon in *The Bulletin* of a conversation with Packer immediately prior to Mahogany's storming run in the 1993 Victoria Derby.

'Hey, Greggie, do you think this horse will win or not?' Packer had asked.

'Yep. How much you had on it, KP?'

'$600,000-odd.'

'It will win by a minute.'

Packer raced off and put another million on it.

Many of his reported splurges naturally involved his own horses. But some didn't, as Hall explained of his win six years earlier in the 1987 Sydney Cup, on a Packer/Williams chestnut named Major Drive. It was his first victory for Packer and he

'You know there were two Kerry Packers. The one before he sold Channel Nine would limit himself to back a horse to win $500,000, but the Kerry Packer after he sold the network, it seemed the sky was the limit.'

Bookie Bruce McHugh, 'Bookie recalls millions of reasons Packer went racing', Patrick Bartley, *The Age*, 28 October 2008.

· ·

'Good. Go and put two hundred and fifty grand on it,' [Packer] instructed.

'That will be a bit of a task, boss, that's a lot of money,' I said.

'It will be less of a task if you stop talking and get on with it,' he replied.

Ken Callander, *Good Luck and Good Punting*

· ·

It was even bigger at Rosehill on Golden Slipper day in 1987. The on-course bookmakers' turnover figures on Golden Slipper day in 1986 figure was $8.2 million, yet the following year they had soared to $40.5 million.

When asked to explain the remarkable 'blip' in the bookmakers' turnover figures, then STC chief executive Pat Parker simply said: 'That was the day Kerry came to the races.'

'THE BIG FELLA AND THE POWER OF THE PUNT', TONY BOURKE, *THE AGE*, 30 DECEMBER 2005

'He kept chasing. He always knew how to get out [on top]. He nearly always got out ... He's not the sort of client you want to talk to every day, but I'll miss him.'

Victorian bookmaker Michael Eskander, who took many big-dollar bets from Packer, quoted in *The Bulletin*, 4 January 2006

Packer had asked me to put $40,000 on a horse for him at Rosehill races in Sydney and I had just explained to him that I couldn't. 'Ian Chappell and Mike Gibson (the two Wide World of Sports hosts) will be crossing to me in about 90 seconds; I won't have time to put your bets on or they will be crossing to an empty screen,' I told the boss.

That is how the 'Who owns the TV station?' quote came about, and needless to say, when I heard it I went straight down and put the bet on.

Wouldn't you? I needed the wages.

And, exactly as I feared, when Mike Gibson said 'Here's Kenny Callander at Rosehill', nobody was there.

NINE'S RACING COMMENTATOR KEN CALLANDER, *GOOD LUCK AND GOOD PUNTING*

'I said, "Kerry, I'm going to go broke or you're going to have a heart attack. Let's put a limit on bets that only allows you to back one to win $2 million." He agreed and on the first race at Flemington that afternoon, he had $2 million to $500,000, another $2 million to $600,000 in Brisbane and an even million dollars on the first favourite in Adelaide.

'After they went down, Kerry came over to me ... it was ... rather daunting ... seeing this huge man looking down over his glasses and saying, "This is no fucking fun any more, I'm changing the rules. I want an even $6 million on the next favourite in Melbourne."'

Bookie Bruce McHugh, quoted in 'Bookie recalls millions of reasons Packer went racing', Patrick Bartley, *The Age*, 28 October 2008.

later found himself in Packer's Bellevue Hill home, basking in the warmest hospitality of the Big Fella ... Who, it turned out, hadn't actually backed Major Drive, but had $6 million at 6-4 on, on the favourite Myocard, which had run second.

Packer's spree over a frightening fortnight of Autumn Carnival in 1987 still makes bookmakers swoon. At the Golden Slipper at Rosehill, exactly two weeks before the Sydney Cup, Packer lost as much as $7 million on his horse Christmas Tree, according to Eric Connolly, veteran racing editor of Sydney's *Daily Telegraph*. The bookmakers' holdings from that weekend were double those of the previous year.

Indeed, Packer was said to have bet more than $100 million over the 1987 Autumn Carnival, scoring some wins to offset his better-publicised losses.

In another well-publicised Packer turf splurge, during the 1991 AJC Easter Racing Carnival, 'Buckets' is said to have spilled $55 million to Sydney bookmaker Bruce McHugh— one of few bookies able to man-up to Packer's punts. McHugh later revealed that Packer, in an attempt to foil the racing media that followed his every move, code-named a million-dollar bet a 'brick'.

McHugh retired from bookmaking just two days after the 1991 carnival. He went on to become a long-serving chairman of the Sydney Turf Club. Although, it could be argued he'd already given something back to the club, particularly during that 1991 carnival.

'Nobody anywhere in the world, before or after, has ever paid as much turnover tax,' McHugh told the *Sydney Morning Herald* in 2011, of his 1991 Packer play. 'I paid the Australian Jockey Club $1 million and Treasury $1 million, for one week. And I was in bookmaking for 20 years.'

Packer made some notably enormous punts on the Melbourne Cup, in league with Melbourne mate Williams. Their $2 million on the nose of Might and Power in 1997 made the papers, and the pair picked a winner again in 1998 with Jezabeel, winning more than $5 million, according to *The Bulletin*.

There may well be incalculable remnants of Packer's punting sprees sown into the turf and lining the clubrooms of Australia's most ritzy racecourses. But one especially coveted souvenir is the trophy for the Doncaster Mile, held annually at Royal Randwick in Sydney since 1866.

It was crafted in England and presented in 1858 to the winner of the original Doncaster Cup, the oldest continuously run horse race in the world, held at the English racecourse of the same name.

Kerry Packer purchased the trophy in the late 1970s and brought it back to donate to the AJC. He requested that it be used as the trophy for the Frank Packer Plate, which commenced in 1980. Since 2009, however, with the Packer family's permission, the trophy—estimated to be worth $250,000—has been presented to the winner of the Doncaster Mile.

In 2012, the winner was a horse named More Joyous. In celebrating the victory, her high-profile owner grabbed the precious trophy and thrust it into the air—causing the lid and base to separate and come crashing to the ground. Packer would have been laughing in his grave, as the winning owner was his old mate, Sydney advertising and media man John Singleton.

'I went to pick it up thinking, 17th-century real silver, it's going to weigh a tonne. But I think it's Alfoil,' Singo joked. 'I think I've uncovered an insurance fraud here ... Ros Packer has got the real one at home. I'm not saying Ros has perpetrated the crime, but one of the maids.'

'[A Packer pal] wanted me to put this money—ten grand I think it was—on this horse for him in Brisbane. Reckoned it was a real good thing. Said I should put something on the horse myself. I don't know why—I can't really explain it—but I felt something wasn't right. I sensed something. I didn't feel good about it. I said to the bloke: "No, I'm sorry, I don't think I want to put that money on for you. Get someone else to put it on." Know the name of the horse? Fine *bloody* Cotton.'

Kerry Packer as quoted by Garry Linnell, on how his instincts saved him from one of Australian turf's greatest scandals, the Fine Cotton ring-in controversy in 1984. *The Bulletin*, 4 January 2006

'Packer liked horses but he preferred to ride them. Racecourses, you sensed, bored him. Not the races themselves, and certainly not the punt, but the humbug between races, the socialising and coat-tugging, the strutting and posing ... Packer liked thoroughbreds well enough but they were, first of all, animals to bet on, even his derby, cup and Golden Slipper winners.'

LES CARLYON, 'A GIANT AMONG MEN', *THE BULLETIN*, 4 JANUARY 2006

'They'd tip me the horses they were riding. I'd put the money on and they'd get a sling—a pretty generous one, too—if the horse won ... Nearly everything they tipped me was a nine or 10 [chance to win] ... Then I realised what was wrong. The bloody jockeys weren't risking anything. Cheeky little buggers. They tipped me these horses. If the horses won, the jockeys got money—on no outlay, mind you—and if they lost, the jockeys lost nothing. I was the mug. So I figured out a new system ... I'd say ... "So, if it's such a certainty, you'll want to back it yourself, won't you? You put a grand in my hand and I'll put on two grand for you. But you've got to put the money in my hand first!"... And they'd say: "Well, jeez Kerry, I think he'll go good—but there are no certainties in this game."'

KERRY PACKER AS QUOTED BY GARRY LINNELL, *THE BULLETIN*, 4 JANUARY 2006

[Packer's secretary] Pat Wheatley dabbled in horse racing and was a part-owner of Sound Horizon, which won the rich Epsom Handicap in 1987.

When she asked for time off to watch the horse at its first start, Packer lectured her on the perils of a young woman owning a racehorse—then told her to put $1000 on for him.

The horse failed to win and Packer could scarcely conceal his glee. Wheatley shot back: 'Well, you should laugh; I put your thousand on the nose.'

She was joking; it was part of the banter they shared.

'Packer's Miss Moneypenny', obituary of Pat Wheatley 26 October 2008, David Haselhurst, *The Age*, 30 October 2008

8

SPORTING AMBITION

From a sickly childhood (contracting polio at age seven), and struggling with dyslexia, Kerry Packer focused more on sport than his schooling and grew up to be a competent sort of sportsman. At Geelong Grammar, he was school heavyweight boxing champion, played cricket in the first XI, rugby in the first XV and was also headlong into golf, tennis and swimming.

This era of intensive school sport would equip him with not only a passion for sport, but with a rich, deep seam of sporting ability that could be mined even decades later, when he was far from physically fit.

Packer quit drinking alcohol at just 18, after being involved in a multiple-fatality road accident, but he was evidently unable to maintain similar abstinence (or even moderation) in his smoking or diet.

At age 40, Packer's bold World Series Cricket initiative suddenly put him in the centre of a global sports spotlight. He stepped up admirably, taking on a challenge in London in August 1977, at the height of his stand-off against the International Cricket Conference, to play in an England versus Australia media game.

'I think you qualify' (as Australian media), Ian Chappell had wryly observed.

During the game, Packer batted a couple of singles and then stepped in as wicket-keeper. There, he had the not inconsiderable satisfaction of catching out Peter Lush of the Test and County Cricket Board.

'He had a bit of ability,' recalls Greg Chappell. His brother Ian would also sing the praises of the WSC boss. 'He loved talking about cricket and talking about sport. That was why it was a pleasure to work for him, because you knew he wasn't just a television magnate churning out product.'

During the High Court case against the ICC a month later, Packer admitted: 'Contrary to public opinion, I have always liked cricket. I have always been a little resentful of the fact that I was never coached properly.'

Years later, television host Ray Martin would tell of a charity match between Channels Nine and Seven. Packer, batting with Nine's music director Geoff Harvey, proceeded to knock nearly a century in fours and sixes, while refusing to run for singles.

Some of those cricketing skills would have been kept in tune by the infamous baseball-pitching machine that Packer had had installed in Bellevue Hill. It was reportedly a weekly event for Packers *pere et fils*, along with various invited cricket stars, to face the machine's deliveries at a V-max of around 190 kilometres per hour.

Kerry had refused to let James' cricket coach Barry Knight turn down the speed, saying 'What are you trying to do, turn him into a wuss? Come on, turn it up a bit!' West Indies captain Clive Lloyd refused to take on the machine which, after all, could hurl a ball 30 kilometres per hour faster than any human ever has. Packer, naturally, manned up—and was at least once laid out flat by the missile-launching machine.

The body may not have always been up to it, but the spirit burned undiminished. Christopher Forsyth's *The Great Cricket Hijack*, quotes Packer as saying 'I would have given my eye teeth to be a champion.'

Former Australian Rugby League chairman Ken Arthurson had a privileged and very personal insight during the 1993 announcement of Nine's acquisition of the League's broadcast rights. The two men were standing in the centre of the playing field at the Sydney Cricket Ground.

During an interview with Packer, *A Current Affair* host Ray Martin asked, 'Would you have given anything to have played for Australia?'.

'Absolutely,' replied Packer.

'In what sport?' asked Martin.

Packer didn't hesitate: 'Anything. Marbles.'

'Is this course for sale? Because I do intend playing and if I have to buy it, well, that's not out of the question.'

Kerry Packer's response to a golf club's refusal to let him play, as he was wearing a shirt without a collar (as told by Alan Jones at Packer's memorial service, 17 February 2006

'He turned to me with a sort of faraway look in his eyes,' Arthurson told *The Bulletin*. 'Ya know, I'd give just about anything to have played a grand final here ... Or a cricket Test.' He meant it, too. You could just tell he meant it.'

By that stage, in 1995, Packer had endured 10 years of peaks and troughs in his physical condition. In 1986, he had collapsed on a Scottish golf course and was rushed to London, where he had his gall bladder and a cancerous kidney removed. Either one of these operations, you'd hope, would be a once-in-a-lifetime experience. The London doctors told Packer he had better find something sporting to do, or he was a dead man walking.

Packer had a broad catalogue of sporting interests to investigate.

At various times, he'd fancied himself as a big-game hunter. Tony Greig told one story of Packer enticing him to the Okavango Delta in Botswana. Other Packer pals also told of raucous roo and pig-shooting trips in the Northern Territory and Kimberley.

He was certainly fond of, and very knowledgeable about firearms. He was said to keep a fair collection of guns at home in Bellevue Hill, and presumably wasn't short of weapons on the rural property at Ellerston, 350km north of Sydney.

When it came to horses, though, Packer's own daughter Gretel described him as a 'complete softie'. He'd enjoyed an affinity with the animals since his childhood, and maintained a close relationship through his thoroughbred partnerships with property developer and fellow big punter, Lloyd Williams. Gretel told the *Australian Women's Weekly* after her father's passing, 'Dad loved his horses and they loved him.'

Jodhi Meares, married to James Packer from 1999–2002, recalled a situation that showed Kerry's compassion for horses. The incident, which she related during interviews for the ABC

TV's *Australian Story* in 2014, occurred as the Packer clan was driving to Tullamarine airport after the running of the Melbourne Cup.

A horse float had jackknifed on the freeway, leaving one of the horses trapped in the upturned float and the other running terrified on the road.

'We drove past exactly as this was happening and I was like "Oh, stop the car," and, you know, just saw this horse running down the middle of traffic. So of course Kerry told his driver to stop the car and we all got out.

'James went and caught the other horse and helped calm it down. And Kerry was dealing with the situation with the float that had been turned over and he called somebody and said "we need a hacksaw …"

'I think it was 30 or 40 minutes and the whole situation had sort of been handled and he'd got the horse free. I didn't see anyone else stopping, you know what I mean? They stopped, and it was just the right thing to do.'

Perhaps it was with horses at heart, then, that Packer decided his grand sporting passion would be polo. It's understood that while still in London recuperating from the gall bladder and kidney surgery, he got on the phone to legendary Australian grazier and former 10-goal polo player, Sinclair Hill.

Hill is a larger-than-life figure in the Australian bush, known for his uncanny ability to 'read' rural property from the air and his forthright opinions on government and, well, anything. Yet Hill is far more than a gruff, one-dimensional cattleman: an old-school gentleman, he once coached a young Prince Charles in polo. Decades later, Prince Harry worked as a jackaroo on a Queensland cattle station owned by Hill's son.

In 1986, Hill had been retired from polo for 11 years. He was 52 years old; Packer, 48. But Hill must have sensed that a sport Packer actually liked, one that might actually hold his attention and keep him coming back, could literally mean the difference between life and death. And so 'Kerro' had himself a polo coach.

Packer very quickly had everything imaginable to go with it. Within a year, his new recreational pursuit was accelerated

In 1999, *Business Review Weekly* reported a conversation between Kerry Packer and rag-trade baron Sam Gazal, in which Packer asked Gazal how much he thought he could live on each year. Gazal picked a figure: $200,000.

Packer responded, 'I'm the same. I'm a simple bloke, I only need a couple of hundred grand a year.'

Cue son James, who said: 'Try $105 million, like last year.'

'They brought out these polo ponies that were worth about $30–40,000 each ... I remember being on this horse ride and looking over at the golf course. I said, "Man, how large is that green?" It was just beautifully manicured. And the guy said, "Nah, that's the fairway."'

GARRY LINNELL, FORMER EDITOR OF *THE BULLETIN*, ON AN EXECUTIVE RETREAT AT ELLERSTON

by another once-in-a-lifetime experience: Alan Bond. Packer said to John D'Arcy of the *Herald & Weekly Times*, 'I'm going to take three years off and get fit and then I'm going to come back and buy television stations for half the price their new owners just paid for them.'

With typical determination and a no-less-typical torrent of cash, he began to construct world-class polo estates at his Ellerston property in NSW, reportedly with more than 160 horses in air-conditioned stables. Equivalent facilities were established in England (Stedham, near his Fyning Hill estate), 'Ellerstina' in Argentina, and a smaller estate in France.

Biographer Paul Barry estimated that Packer burned through close to $150 million on this new obsession, which quickly extended to two teams: Ellerston Black and Ellerston White. Packer's ongoing outlay didn't only include the costs of breeding, keeping and transporting horses, but the no less testosterone-fuelled demands of professional Argentinian polo players, who would travel with Packer and James through the calendar of tournaments in Spain, France, England, Argentina and Australia.

Packer's heart attack during the 1990 Australian Open Polo Championship in Sydney, covered in Chapter 10, did not dampen his enthusiasm for the game; he returned to Warwick Farm the very next weekend to watch James play. He continued to push himself to even higher levels, while equally channelling his efforts into the breeding of ponies and the development of his estates.

His Ellerstina venture near Buenos Aries, Argentina with polo patriarch Gonzalo Pieres was revolutionary in the manner and scale of its embryo programs and player training camps. Ellerstina has won Argentina's prestigious Open six times, the first three of those in Packer's lifetime (1994, 1997 and 1998).

The 38-hectare Great House Farm complex in Stedham, West Sussex was likewise a formidable, purpose-built polo complex. It was sold in 1999. The nearby Fyning Hill was sold in 1990 for £12 million to Russian businessman Roman Abramovich. This 178-hectare estate was said to include a seven-bedroom house, stables for 100 horses, two polo pitches and a go-kart track.

Packer watched his son James's Ellerston Black team win the British Open Gold Cup in 1994, and he led his own Ellerston White team to victory in 1995 and 1998. Polo led to the rough diamond from down-under winning the Queen's Cup, presented on more than one occasion by Queen Elizabeth II herself.

Daughter Gretel told the *Australian Women's Weekly* after her father's passing, 'He loved that it's like chess on horseback; a game of strategy and skill, and both an individual and a team game. He loved that he could be on the same field as the best in the world.'

John Bary, a former six-goal professional polo player, left no doubt of Packer's polo legacy. After his retirement in 2011, Bary told Melbourne's *Herald Sun*: 'The big money is overseas in polo, but Mr Packer lifted the bar and did a lot of service to the sport in New Zealand and Australia.'

Ellerston's polo facilities are said to be second to none in Australia. If it's second to any in the southern hemisphere, it would only be Ellerstina in Argentina. It has as many as eight polo pitches, an oval racecourse, hi-tech stable facilities and an equine hospital.

Packer, aside from his commendable polo conquests, enjoyed playing golf, and in the mid-1970s was able to benefit from some pro lessons. This meant owning the course—The Australian, in Sydney—and picking up tips on swing and stance from Jack Nicklaus.

Packer would also get a good-sized glimpse of what it was to be a champion golfer. In 1992, he was invited to play in the AT&T Pro-Am tournament, the world's most prestigious pro-am event, held at Pebble Beach near Monterey, in Northern California.

He had played pro-ams before—one, in Ohio in 1978, partnered with Jack Nicklaus, former president Gerald Ford and comedian Bob Hope—and the Pebble Beach event at least once before, in 1979, again with Nicklaus. For 1992 he would partner fellow Australian Greg Norman, at the time usually ranked among the top three in the world. The two had known each other from a meeting eight years earlier at The Australian golf club in Sydney.

Packer hadn't been spending much time on golf, and he took the 1992 challenge seriously. In Sydney he had Ron Luxton, the long-serving pro at The Australian, help him tune up his swing. Then he flew in Mitchell Spearman, golf instructor from the hugely exclusive Lake Nona Country Club in Orlando, Florida. Spearman spent two weeks in Sydney giving private lessons.

Norman and Packer strode to victory by six shots, shooting a 42 under par. Packer, with his handicap, contributed 38 of their under-par shots. Their 246 remains the second-lowest winning score in Pebble Beach Pro-Am history.

But more than Packer's playing, it was something that happened just prior to the game that had truly impressed Greg Norman. In the days after Packer's death in 2005, Norman told the story to veteran *Sydney Morning Herald* golf writer, Peter Stone.

'We walked onto the first tee to hit off and they had Kerry's handicap down as 21. "Kerry, is that your handicap?" "No, it's 18," he replied. That's the character of the man. Most amateurs would have said "I'll take the 21," saying, "Shit, OK, great, I'll take the extra shots." But Kerry, with his high morals and high ethics, said no and we won by six shots.

'To see Kerry as happy as he was at the end of the day, that's what life is about. Achieving that. Money doesn't buy that stuff.'

After the match, the US-based *Golf World* asked Packer how it felt to win the event, compared with closing a big business deal. 'This costs more,' Packer quipped.

Greg Norman would soon become more entwined in Packer's golfing life, as all—or certainly most—of Packer's sporting dreams culminated in the haven he created for himself and his family at Ellerston.

Arguably the jewel of Ellerston is the golf course that Packer commissioned from Greg Norman, as he and then business partner Bob Harrison moved increasingly into golf course design. It hosted its first game in 2001.

Norman explained in *The Bulletin*'s tribute issue to Packer that the catalyst had been a strange theory put forward by the proprietor. 'Kerry always had a belief that any golf course in the world could be played using a putter. It might take several hundred shots to get around, but he believed there was no course that could defy his putter theory. So he wanted one that could.'

Co-designer Harrison, who left Greg Norman Golf Course Design in 2009, explained the process to *Planet Golf USA*: 'The first task was to work out where to put the golf course on a 75,000 acre property. The manager … wasn't a golfer and thought that the best place for the course was probably on top of the extremely steep ridges. But there was a beautiful, fast-flowing stream in the valley below, where I thought the course should go—and much of it did—even though it meant moving the polo ponies to new pastures and building a number of extensive bridges to link the paddocks beside the creek.'

Harrison had also said that the course, which might see half a dozen rounds played on it each week, was designed for experienced players. 'It was done specifically for the Packer family and they can hit the ball,' he said.

The Great White Shark himself said: 'At Ellerston we were able to create a course that a golfer of my calibre would love to play every day for the rest of his life.'

Greg Norman, who became a close friend of Packer's, would have bittersweet memories of Ellerston, and the world-class golf course that they'd built together over many determined discussions.

'My greatest regret,' Norman told *The Bulletin* after his friend's death, 'is that we didn't do it 20 years earlier, as I never got to play a round with him. When I played, he'd come around in the cart.'

'He'd always
say it didn't
matter what
he did—people
would still
resent him for
his wealth.
If you want
to envy Kerry
Packer, be
jealous instead
of his lust for
life.'

Greg Norman, *The Bulletin*, 4 January 2006

'Oh, doesn't it fucking go!'

Kerry Packer to Kevin Bartlett, on his modified Jaguar XJ-S which had twice as much power as a contemporary Formula 1 car

9

PACKER'S TOYS

It was the late 1970s. The jungle drums of Sydney's petrol-head scene rumbled with sightings of a mythical wild cat. It was low, loud, with the power of two Formula 1 cars and a muscled-up body that bulged rudely over tyres as fat as a tractor's. One report, claiming to know the whereabouts of its lair, said the beast spat fire at anyone who went near it.

For all that, the beast was only as mysterious and fearsome as its rumoured owner: Packer.

The man behind the world's most expensive, powerful, unreliable and inflammable Jaguar XJ-S was Kevin Bartlett. A multiple Australian motor racing champion and engineer, Bartlett was a versatile and aggressive charger in single-seat formula machines and touring cars, both here and abroad.

According to a story related in Christopher Lee's *Howzat! Kerry Packer's War*, Packer may have succumbed to the XJS's Rubenesque charms while in London during the September, 1977 High Court case against his World Series Cricket. Packer and his controversial WSC signatory, Tony Greig visited a Jaguar showroom to look at the car.

Packer asked the salesman about the colour availability. On being told there were five hues from which to choose, Packer ordered one of each, and distributed four of them among his favoured executives.

Jaguar had launched the XJ-S in 1975, as the replacement for its fabled E-Type. Jaguar's V12 engine produced a reasonable

220 kilowatts (295 horsepower), but the XJ-S's size, weight and thirst relegated it to the role of a posh *boulevardier* aimed at the American market.

Packer suggested that Bartlett might do something to make his XJ-S go faster. Bartlett, who raced hairy-chested, 375kW (500 horsepower) Formula 5000s around the world, reasoned that if this was worth doing, it was worth *over*-doing.

Bartlett had met Packer around 1979 when the race ace received a call asking if he'd be willing to give some driving lessons to Mr Packer. Bartlett suggested the Oran Park race circuit, south-west of Sydney.

'We hopped in the car, I think it was the XJ-S and I took him around,' recalls Bartlett.

'After a little while he said: "Enough of this. I want to have a run around, you tell me what I'm doing wrong"...

'I've often thought the reason we hit it off was that I was actually telling him what to do. That can only lead so far with Packer before he says, "Well, fuck—don't tell *me* to do it that way!"

'I said, "If I tell you to do something, it's because you need to know the next step. If you can't do it the way I want you to, you just go and do your own thing. And when you crash, don't fuckin' blame me."

'I knew who he was, but to me he was just a rich businessman. He said, "Do you know who you're talking to?" "Yeah, I'm talking to a bloke I'm trying to teach how to drive" ... So he said, "Alright then, show me!" And it went on from there.'

On the circuit, Bartlett says, he could readily see that Packer 'was quite a good steerer', with a flair for driving quickly.

Bartlett also recognised he was getting some respect.

'Once we'd got over that argumentative stage, which didn't last long—he was a very forgiving guy, in a lot of ways—it turned out it wasn't a mistake to be that insistent. What he respected was that I'd stuck to my guns.'

Packer, it seemed, was happy—or at least able—to defer to others who were expert in their particular field and had the confidence to assert it. Thus, characters like helicopter pilot Nick Ross, polo mentor Sinclair Hill, cattleman Ken Warriner and a small circle of others, became trusted confidants.

Bartlett found himself propelled into that inner circle as the go-to guy for motoring matters. In short order, Bartlett would be servicing Packer's cars at his Sydney race workshop, jetting off to source high-powered toys, accompanying him on automotive adventures, designing a go-kart track for the Ellerston property and, most visibly, carrying Channel Nine sponsorship on his Formula 5000 and Chevrolet Camaro racing cars.

The adventure would run until the end, 25 years later.

But back to the beginning and the fire-breathing Jag.

A new technology, among passenger cars at least, was the turbocharger: a turbine pump that crams ever greater quantities of fuel and air into the engine, creating prodigious power—for so long as the engine can take the pressure.

'I said, we'll put a couple of turbochargers on it,' Bartlett grins. 'But it was a complete and utter bloody disaster, the whole way along ...

'We estimated it got up to about 1200 horsepower [895kW], before we backed it off to about 800,' Bartlett says. 'You couldn't drive it very often—you couldn't drive it around the city because it was a complete dog, and that's what Packer didn't like about it. The carburettors would jam and then the car would catch fire.

'It never caught fire with him in it, thankfully. But it did with me, a couple of times.'

It was a work in progress. Bartlett strove to resolve the issues of delivering fuel, keeping the engine cool, and strengthening the transmission system to handle the power of two contemporary F1 cars. And between times, having to blast it with a fire extinguisher and clean it all up again.

'Then one day he rang me—or his secretary rang me—and said, "KP wants to go down to Canberra, is the XJ-S ready?" I said, "Well, it is." She said, "Go up to the house to collect him and you can go down to Canberra." I thought: "Shit"...'

Bartlett was understandably less than confident of the big Jag's ability to make the trip—around four hours, prior to today's freeway—without self-immolating.

'So I picked him up, and he said, "I've got to get to Canberra in an hour and a half, two hours tops." I said, "Well, we won't do it in this." He said, "Why the fuck not? You said you just tuned the fuckin' thing up, why won't it do it?" I said we've never done that sort of distance before … "Just hop in the fuckin' thing and shut up, I've gotta get to Canberra."'

At the wheel of the Jag and thundering up to speed, Packer instructed Bartlett to phone the office and have his helicopter dispatched to follow them. The Jag had a head start of about 35 kilometres when the chopper lifted off from Channel Nine.

'We get to Mittagong,' Bartlett says (a distance of 115 kilometres from Sydney) 'and Christ alone knows how many police cars were after us by that time. I wasn't looking at the speedo, but we were going hard, *waaa-waaaa*, top-gear stuff. And suddenly he says, "I haven't seen that chopper. They're supposed to monitor where I am. Where's the fuckin' chopper?"'

'There wasn't much phone coverage in those days, and I had to ring someone and get them to ring someone. Eventually, somebody says: "The chopper pilot says he can see you in the distance, but *they can't catch you!*"'

By Mittagong, Bartlett was panicking that the Jag would set a signal fire for them. 'The thing was starting to smoke, the gearbox was smelly and I thought, ohh, shit … I said look, I've just got to pull up and check the gearbox oil … He said, "But I've gotta get to rah-rah-rah," but I explained that we wouldn't get there if the gearbox blew up.

'Naturally, it was pissing oil everywhere, I was waiting for it to catch fire again, and he says, "I'm not gonna make Canberra in this, am I?" So I phoned the chopper and we got to somewhere near the Bong Bong Racetrack … the guys landed in farmer Fred's paddock, and Packer's over the fence and off. "See you in Canberra!" he says.'

Bartlett did make it to the house on Mugga Lane, albeit several hours behind the car's owner. 'He said, "Oh, you got it here," and I said yeah, but I took it pretty easy. And he said, "Well that's not what I'm fuckin' payin' for, is it?"'

Packer kept the Jaguar for perhaps five or six years. Bartlett says that pretty much every time he took the car out, something else would break. The car became almost useful the more they scaled back the engine power, settling on that of just one Formula 1 car. Then it caught fire again.

The burnt-out Jag was salvaged and rebuilt to fight another day. There was a popular story that the subsequent owner, Sydney Jaguar mechanic Gary Walker, had a favourite trick of sticky-taping one end of a $50 note to the glove box lid and challenging a passenger, under the full force of the Jag's acceleration, to try and retrieve it.

But Bartlett is convinced that, for all the angst caused by the Jaguar, Packer enjoyed the entire saga.

Why not just buy a Ferrari, or a Porsche 911 Turbo? 'Oh no, he wouldn't do that. It had to be an individual thing, a *him* thing.'

'IF IT'S THAT FUCKIN' GOOD, WE'LL HAVE IT. AND IF WE CAN'T REGISTER IT, WE'LL LEAVE IT UP AT ELLERSTON.'

Kerry Packer on the imported left-hand drive
Audi Quattro, which didn't comply with
Australian rules and couldn't be road registered.

OUT OF THE AUDINARY

Audi is today one of the most respected players in the luxury car market. But back in 1980, few Australians had even heard of it, or had reason to pay any attention if they had. Audi's, certainly weren't the sort of cars to excite a car-mad tycoon homing in on a nine-figure net worth.

In March 1980, however, at the Geneva Motor Show, Audi unveiled the Quattro. The muscular, high-performance coupe was revolutionary in that it featured four-wheel drive, a technology previously focused on plodding, off-road utility vehicles.

Four-wheel drive made this turbocharged coupe uncatchable in wet, slippery or gravel road conditions—the playgrounds of the tough sport of forest rallying.

News of the game-changing, all-wheel drive Audi crackled through to the Australian specialist car magazines. But it was soon clear that the Quattro, being built only for the European market, would be yet another in a long line of exotic cars that would forever elude Australian buyers.

Well, all but one Australian, who had the clout to hijack a car and enlist the help of Audi's top engineers to rebuild it.

In early 1981, Kevin Bartlett received a call from Audi's Australian public relations manager, Phil Scott (who would, much later, become publisher at Packer's ACP). Scott was staring at a physical example of the Quattro, diverted through Sydney en route to a dealership in Madagascar.

The silver car was in left-hand drive, and hence not strictly road-legal, but Scott cheekily suggested they take it for a spin. In 1981, the car's grip around corners, coupled with its turbocharged performance, was astonishing even to the hardened race driver.

Bartlett recalls that, a matter of days later, he was in Packer's office when Packer asked: 'What's new that's any bloody good? I need something for up at Ellerston.'

Bartlett gushed about the Audi, explaining that it had just made every other performance coupe obsolete. 'Uh-huh, well, we'd better have one of them,' Packer grunted.

Bartlett began to explain that this car already had a Madagascan owner, that it didn't comply with Australian rules, it couldn't be road registered ...

Next thing Bartlett knew, he was in Germany, meeting senior Audi engineer Roland Gumpert. It was not unlike being granted an audience with Enzo Ferrari. Bartlett arranged the trip, but it was all, naturally, on the boss's dime.

Doesn't matter what it costs. Just do it right.

'You just go, it will all be there,' Bartlett says. 'Nothing spared, first-class everything ... All of that was taken care of by his secretary [Pat Wheatley]. He trusted me to make decisions as I went along.

'There were times when he asked me, "Why did it cost that much?" And I'd only have to tell him, it was the only way to make it work, and work properly.'

Gumpert and Bartlett sat down and identified all the parts from other Audi models that would enable Bartlett to convert the commandeered Madagascan car to right-hand drive and manoeuvre it through road registration when he got home.

Drives from Sydney to Ellerston, which Packer and Bartlett regularly shared, were much enjoyed by the Big Fella, as they explored the unfamiliar driving technique demanded by the Audi's four-wheel drive system.

'Took him a while,' Bartlett says. 'But it took me a while, too. You had the drive the car really aggressively, pitch it into corners. He got to do it quite well, actually. Nearly all the way from Moonan Flat to Ellerston was on dirt in those days, and he had a bloody ball through there. Always had a big go. He enjoyed his motoring.'

GOING RACING

One of Australia's best-remembered Bathurst racing cars is Kevin Bartlett's 'Channel Nine' Chevrolet Camaro. The dark blue coupe was a constant threat in the early-1980s to the established front-line of Peter Brock's Holdens and Dick Johnson's Fords.

Bartlett had made his name in Formula 5000, Australia's equivalent to Formula 1. The Camaro campaign came about through Bartlett's burgeoning friendship with Kerry Packer.

'[Packer] just said to me one day: "How can you go against these other blokes, this Peter Brock character? You can beat him, can't ya?"' Bartlett grins. 'I said, "Yeah, most probably could—he's been beaten, it might as well be me doing it. But I don't race in that category." He said, "Well, get yourself a car that you can race in that category."'

The obvious choice would have been Holden or Ford, for which there was a ready industry in parts and preparation expertise. Packer suggested that Bartlett try to find something different; Bartlett suspects, to avoid snubbing either of the two local brands that were among Channel Nine's biggest advertisers.

Bartlett began looking at eligible cars with competition potential. In Packer-world, such research wasn't going to be restricted to poring over wads of technical documents in a library.

'That was a round-the-world trip, that one,' Bartlett says. 'I went to Germany, looked at BMW and Mercedes, went to Paris to get all the relevant paperwork ... Then I went to Detroit and bought a Camaro Z28.'

Bartlett began modifying the car to race in the 1979 Bathurst 1000, just four months away. It was a tough schedule. But come the October date, Bartlett would struggle to drive a wheelchair: he was lucky to have survived a 200km/h crash in his F5000 a month earlier.

'I remember it well because it was the ninth of the ninth, 1979, and the car number was nine ... I thought, this doesn't bode too well.'

The crash had ended Bartlett's F5000 career and left him with a lifelong limp.

He continued to develop the Camaro, and was quickly on the pace with it in 1980, taking second in the championship behind Brock. Bartlett qualified the Camaro on pole position at Bathurst in 1980 and again in '81, though the car would not figure highly in the results.

No, the car that Kerry and Kevin built will be best remembered as the 'Channel Six Camaro', for its career-ending 1982 Bathurst race. Bartlett was running with the lead pack when the Camaro's left rear wheel collapsed. The car lurched into the wall and then neatly rolled onto its roof, sliding inverted along the track for some distance before coming to rest.

Back in Sydney, the car's sponsor was relieved to see his driver emerge from the car angry, but unharmed. Whereupon, Packer was said to have taken endless delight in seeing his Nine network's logo—even inverted, as a six— occupying so much of rival Channel Seven's headline sports telecast.

It was a case of one-downmanship and one-upmanship at the same time.

ROAD TEST

A bloke like Kerry Packer didn't go shopping for cars; usually, the cars came shopping for him. But when some new four-wheeled toys piqued his interest, few had better resources immediately at hand. *Wheels*, the nation's best-selling motoring magazine, happened to be among the ACP stable. As, indeed, was the second-biggest seller, *MOTOR*.

In 1990–91 Honda had launched a Ferrari-baiting $160,000 supercar, a slinky, aluminium-bodied missile dubbed the NSX. But around the same time, Nissan decided to import 100 road-going examples of its $110,000 all-wheel drive Skyline GT-R coupe. Dubbed 'Godzilla', this turbo terror was in the midst of trouncing Australia's motor racing scene.

The Honda was like a Ferrari that Packer might conceivably fit into. But the Nissan was thematically similar to his trio of Audi Quattros, and Bartlett had already gushed to the Boss about it.

Everyone was interested in these, and the new breed of supercar. And so it came to pass that the *Wheels* magazine crew arrived just after dawn one Sunday morning at Sydney's Eastern Creek Raceway, armed with its hi-tech Leitz Correvit digital speed-measuring equipment, chief test pilot Kevin Bartlett and a quintet of supercars adding up to just shy of $1 million.

The pressure was on to make the deadline for the May 1991 issue. Getting through five cars in one day, what with performance testing, course set-up, photography and tyre-changing requirements, would demand solid focus.

John Carey, *Wheels*' long-serving road test editor was there:

'I remember that day well. I was setting up cones with KB [Kevin Bartlett] on the straight when this nice chopper ... that was headed in a westerly direction, went into a hover overhead. I asked KB: "Is that who I think it is?" He fessed up that he'd mentioned this to KP, and that he'd been interested ...

'He was on his way with a bunch of polo players to a tournament in Richmond or Windsor, with young James in tow,

'Someone at *Wheels* magazine phoned [a prominent Sydney Honda dealer] about borrowing a car. "*Wheels*? Why would I do anything for you? Thanks to you bastards, Kerry Packer cancelled his order for two NSXs ..."'

JOHN CAREY, *WHEELS* LONG-SERVING ROAD TEST EDITOR

too. We had a Honda NSX, Nissan Skyline GT-R, a privately-owned Ferrari 348tb, a BMW M5 and a Porsche Carrera 4.'

Carey recalls that the big boss drove everything except for the Ferrari, and that James was similarly like a kid in a candy store. But another *Wheels* crew member who was present recalls that the biggest stress-generators were the Argentinian polo players, who were hooning and spinning off the track.

'KP was in and out of the cars that most interested him, the GT-R and the NSX,' Carey recalls. Carey was crouching by the door of the Honda, wrestling with the suction-cups and retainer straps that secured the large timing sensor to the door of the car, when a looming presence seemed to suck out all ambient light.

'KP had stopped to ask me what the Correvit was. So I gave him a quick description of what it did and what it had cost. Which was, in round figures, $50,000.

'"And who owns it?" he asked me.

'"Well, I suppose you do."

'Made him laugh. Nice big one. Genuine. Wealth can make some people into miserable buggers. Not Kerry Packer. He really knew how to enjoy money.'

Packer had been mightily impressed by the Nissan which, aside from its performance, offered a more accommodating cabin than the low-slung, two-seater Honda. Bartlett was standing by the chopper as Packer climbed on board to depart.

'Get me one of those cars,' Packer motioned towards the Nissan. 'Nah, fuck it—get me two. One for James and one for me.'

TASMANIA BEDEVILLED

In 1988, the BMW 750iL was about the most lavishly equipped, complex and expensive car on the Australian market. But the V12-engined limousine was no less impressive in its ability to burn money: a car bought for $216,000 in 1988 (when the average house price in Sydney was $141,000) could dump half its value in just three years.

It's probably for this latter reason, rather than any particular affection, that a white, 1988 BMW 750iL, carrying the FP-222 registration plates of his late father, would be Kerry Packer's automotive staple for the last 17 years of his life. Regularly schmoozed by BMW and other luxury brands, Packer's attitude remained: 'What's wrong with this one?'

But the Packer predilection for performance cars, evidenced by his Jaguar and Audi, had a final, courageous chapter to run, in one of the world's most dangerous and demanding road races.

Packer had bought two Nissan GT-Rs, and in true KP style, was soon asking Bartlett: 'How can we get them going quicker? How much power do you reckon we can get out of them?'

Bartlett shrugged. 'They've got 280 horsepower now. I reckon we can get 450. Piece of cake.'

At that time, 1991, the Nissan GT-R was wiping the floor in Australian motor racing, humiliating the traditional favourite Holdens and Fords. And the fastest Nissan GT-Rs in the world were being built in Melbourne by Bartlett's old racing pal, Fred Gibson.

The instruction was straightforward: 'It wasn't, "How much are you going to charge me, Freddie?" It was, "These engines are for Mr Packer, do it right."'

Packer was delighted with his monster-powered Godzilla toys. He suddenly indicated he'd like a third Nissan GT-R, similarly high-powered, for his Fyning Hill estate in England. Bartlett offered to look into the shipping process.

'What's wrong with this one?'

Kerry Packer, on his 1988 BMW 750iL which he kept for the last
17 years of his life. Packer was regularly being schmoozed by luxury car
brands to upgrade

'I'M NOT COMIN' DOWN TO DRIVE SOME LOW-HORSEPOWER CAR. YOU DRIVE IT.'

Packer to Kevin Bartlett, after being told that the replacement GT-R available to race in the Targa Tasmania 'only' had 350 horsepower.

Packer: 'Nah. I want the thing there next week.' Mere days later, Bartlett was sitting in a first-class seat on a Qantas 747 Combi, a red Nissan GT-R on the same flight with him.

At Heathrow, Bartlett was told that this Australian-specification model did not meet local regulations; thus began a frantic overnight scramble to the Channel Isles, where one may often find alternative solutions to such nettlesome matters.

'With KP, it wasn't a case of, "How much will it cost?" It was a case of, "Why haven't you got it done yet?"' Bartlett says.

'You were put on the mark, you knew you had to perform because you would let the bloke down if you didn't. That's the way I felt about it: I didn't want to let the bloke down, because he trusted me to do what he asked me to do.'

But Packer had another high-stakes goal, involving a powerful Nissan and a small island.

Twelve months earlier, in April 1992, the inaugural Targa Tasmania had been held—a five-day, flat-out road race around the island state. Each year around 300 competitors, flagged away at 30-second intervals, flash along the temporarily closed roads at better than 250 kilometres per hour.

As motor sport adventures go, Targa Tasmania is tough, wild and utterly unforgiving. And Kerry Packer wanted to do it, in one of the most powerful cars in the country.

'He was going to drive a couple of the stages with the GT-R, which I'd arranged at great expense,' Bartlett remembers. 'I took two cars down: one just for practice, one for the event. I had to qualify the car for the event—*big* horsepower—but she went *boom*!'

Packer had been in Sydney, ready to board the chopper the following day to come down to Tasmania. 'And I had the onerous task of ringing him up and saying, "Uh, KP, I've got bad news about the car ..."'

After a response that echoed the Nissan's engine, Packer growled: 'Well, whaddya gonna fuckin' do now?'

Bartlett had, with learned foresight, begun preparing the spare car, which had a 'reasonable' 350 horsepower (indeed, 20 per cent more than the Honda NSX that ultimately won the event) but Packer wasn't impressed.

Bartlett did the event and, despite further mechanical issues, finished third in the Contemporary class. 'But we'd spent $30,000 or so by that time,' Bartlett sighs. 'I knew KP could do it, he was a good enough driver. I felt really bad about it. I said, "I let you down." And he said, "It happened. Let's forget it." But I felt bad about that for years.'

BIG BOYS' TOYS

Kerry Packer in his post-Alan Bond period was a man who took his fun seriously. Where four wheels were concerned, there was one sight more imposing than that of a determined Packer in one of his unholy-horsepower cars: the wheeled man-mountain that was Packer on a 90-kilogram kart, roaring around the dips and twists of Ellerston's custom-made track.

James Packer had Kevin Bartlett design a kart track on a gentle hillside north of the main homestead area.

'James rang me up one day and said, "KB, I want you to build a bloody kart track for me and Dad,"' recalls Bartlett. (James, evidently, had yet to graduate from 'bloody'). The track, ultra-light aircraft and other Ellerston attractions were not only for the benefit of Packers *pere et fils*, but to entertain Argentinian polo players—guys who added a Latin dimension to Attention Deficit Hyperactivity Disorder.

Bartlett was allocated a 1.5 square kilometre area of 'snake-infested' hillside which would, a dozen years later, be among the back nine holes of the golf course. He set to work on a ride-on mower, pegging out the circuit design ready for surfacing.

It was nothing for Bartlett to lob on the doorstep of a Sydney kart shop and buy nine complete K100 championship karts, costing around $2500 each, and a crate of spare parts. Shop owner Peter Dell remembers having to make a new mould for an 'extra-extra-large' seat. He's since used the very same mould for a handful of other plus-sized customers.

A shed was built adjacent to the track to house and maintain the karts. Indeed, maintaining them would become a weekly routine for Bartlett.

'When we were entertaining the Argies, I'd go up nearly every weekend, maintain the karts during the week for a couple of days and then stick around for the weekend. Nick Ross, the helicopter pilot, would wear out a kart every time he'd go up there.'

Garry Linnell, editor of *The Bulletin* from 2002-2006, got to sample the karts on an executive retreat in 2003. Linnell admits he's no racing driver, but was eager to impress the boss.

'I think he had done a 50-something [in seconds lap] around there. I ended up doing some really pathetic lap time. It was embarrassing.'

The Big Man enjoyed the karts immensely, Bartlett says, and was extremely adept at getting the most out of them on the track. 'KP's kart was usually the best, partly because it had the least use,' Bartlett says. 'He'd go and race it around, but he wouldn't wear it out. And his kart didn't have any weight penalty on it. We put weight penalties on all the others, the light blokes went into the heavy karts. But it was never really even.

'James knows quite well that I regarded Kerry as a bloody good driver ... He was always competitive in the karts, and for a big, heavy man—he was using the karts quite hard, and it takes a bit of skill for a heavy man to get a kart to go fast. And I never saw him make a mistake on them. He just had that natural ability.'

The motorised fun didn't stay on the ground, though, as Packer was quick to get onto the new-fangled flying machines called ultra-lights.

He bought six of the spindly, rasping machines—apparently owning a variety of makes, as they were damaged and replaced—though very few guests were qualified to fly them. Trevor Sykes laughs: 'You didn't want to be a guest at Ellerston, because suddenly, with no training whatsoever, you're shoved into one of these things and, "Fly it, you bastard!"'

'Kerry walked over and I said: "So, what sort of time should I be expected to do per lap?"

'And he said, "Anything over 60 seconds, son, and you should be wearing a skirt ..."'

GARRY LINNELL, EDITOR OF *THE BULLETIN* FROM 2002-2006, ON HIS INTRODUCTION TO THE KART TRACK AT ELLERSTON IN 2003

'I've got six ultra-lights (aircraft) out at Ellerston. I'm told it's the most frightening thing you can do. I'm up for a bit of adrenaline—anyone want a go this weekend?'

Kerry Packer to Tony Greig

ON SEA AND AIR

F. Scott Fitzgerald was put on this earth to say it: 'Let me tell you about the very rich. They are different from you and me.' What Fitzgerald didn't say was that the very rich can be different from each other, too.

Among several of the world's wealthiest there has been a long-running battle for supremacy on the high seas. The super-yacht contest has no shortage of high-stakes players. But at the head of the fleet in recent years have been men like tech kings Paul Allen (Microsoft) and Larry Ellison (Oracle), Russian oligarch Roman Abramovich and the expected Middle Eastern and south-east Asian royals.

It's mostly about size: the 180-metre *Azzam*, the largest private superyacht in the world when launched in 2013, is roughly two-thirds the size of the legendary Cunard ocean liner, *Queen Elizabeth II*. Owned by the Emir of Abu Dhabi, *Azzam* usurped the previous size queen, Abramovich's 162 million *Eclipse*, which boasts around 100 rooms, 70 crew, a three-man submarine and space for three helicopters.

But it's also about beauty. The staggering size of these floating palaces is concealed by their sleek and elegant lines, more resembling oversized speedboats than scaled-down ocean liners.

None of this seems to have impressed Packer, when he overcame years of nautical indifference—he had always regarded Sir Frank's sailing exploits as a waste of money—and went looking for a boat.

Packer could have taken the usual route and commissioned a new design from one of the leading German or Italian superyacht specialists. He looked instead to an old and extremely unusual vessel, to be internally transformed and refitted while retaining its original character.

At 87.6 metres in length, *Arctic P* still ranks around 50th in the list of the world's biggest private yachts. Among its sister superyacht fleet, however, Packer's pleasure craft stands out like, er, dogs', for the simple reason that it's an ugly bloody bastard of a boat.

This observation of Genghis Khan—'he wasn't lovable, but he was bloody efficient'—might be applied to *Arctic P*, which began life in 1969 as one of the world's largest ocean-going, ice-classed tugs. Yes, a tugboat. If your 11,000-container super carrier or five-star *Queen Mary 2* breaks down in the north-Atlantic, the *Arctic* is the nuggetty, grimy-faced Charles Bronson character that comes to the rescue.

Packer bought the vessel in 1993 and initiated a year-long, $40 million refit in Malta, during which its interior was transformed into that of a luxury yacht.

Arctic P is said to include accommodation for 12 guests with spa baths in each suite, along with a cinema, indoor swimming pool and the obligatory helipad on the aft deck, along with a sizeable speedboat and a smaller watercraft. She retains a crew of up to 25.

Arctic P's snub nose, low sides, upright superstructure and forest of radar domes and observation towers are the pure antithesis—or the Packer anti-statement—of superyacht styling. But from the sunny shores of Sydney to the ice floes of Alaska, there's virtually nowhere that *Arctic P* need fear to float, and *Boat International* magazine once named her among the world's top five expedition yachts.

Businessmen of Packer's stature need to be able to travel at will. In a one-day round trip from his Sydney office, via chartered plane and helicopters, Packer once personally inked a deal with Rupert Murdoch, who was luxuriating on his 48 million yacht *Morning Glory* in New Zealand's Bay of Islands.

He maintained a small air force of his own, the centrepiece being a McDonnell-Douglas DC-8 that had served its first 16 years as an airliner in the US with United Airlines before passing in 1985 to Hawaiian Airlines. In 1991, 'N897OU'

'I'VE JUST BEEN WAITING FOR THIS MY WHOLE LIFE. A TIE FROM THE FUCKING NEW YORK YACHT CLUB.'

Kerry Packer deadpanning to *Newsweek* executives from New York, at a dinner held at Sydney's Royal Yacht Squadron. According to former ACP advertising executive Graham Lawrence, 'Kerry had never liked the RYS because Frank had spent a lot of money there, with *Gretel I* and *Gretel II*, which was a waste of money as far as Kerry was concerned. These guys thought they were doing a big thing, and he just crunched them.'

was converted to VIP private-jet spec for Packer's Australian Consolidated Press.

This DC-8 was the long-range '62' version, which featured an extra-large wing and forward-raked engine mounts—modifications that gave it a fuel capacity of some 95,500 litres and a range of 7400 nautical miles. By coincidence, or perhaps not, that range accommodated a non-stop flight from Sydney to Las Vegas (around 6700 nautical miles).

Not that he needed to burn his own petrol money: the Vegas casinos maintain their own fleets of biz-jets, to scoop up high rollers when they feel the itch. More than once, Packer was ferried from London in the MGM Grand's Gulfstream V.

According to Paul Barry's *The Rise and Rise of Kerry Packer*, the DC-8 was leased at a cost of $4 million annually, and featured a main bedroom with en suite, a dining table for 12 and separate quarters for the crew. It's also been suggested that Packer's polo ponies were frequent DC-8 flyers.

In 1998 the DC-8, by now re-registered as VP-BLG, was fitted out as a sort of flying hospital to ferry Packer to New York for heart surgery. (The DC-8 left Packer's hands in 2001 and was most recently plane-spotted as the official government jet of the Republic of Togo.)

Meanwhile, Packer's smaller Falcon 200 jet stood in for shorter trips—including, most generously, those for which it was on 24-hour standby on behalf of St Vincent's Hospital in Sydney. Packer had donated the little jet's services for the nationwide collection of organs bound for transplant.

In May 2005, Packer's Falcon 200 had a spot of trouble when it clobbered an errant kangaroo on the runway at Snowy Mountains Airport, near Cooma. The roo caused $400,000 worth of damage to the Falcon's control flaps. It's not known whether Packer was on board at the time, but it's well known that he was angry: Packer claimed that the local shire council was negligent in failing to secure the airport boundary. (In early 2006, just months after KP's passing, James replaced the Falcon 200 with a $61 million Bombardier BD-700 Global Express biz-jet.)

For shorter hops there's never been a substitute for a helicopter, and with the exception of a small Bell 47—presumably relegated to rural duties, along with a pair of Cessna 172s registered to the company—those of the Packer squadron were obviously KP-sized.

One of a pair of prominent Packer-choppers is the Sikorsky S-76B, a $14 million machine capable of seating up to 12 people, and unusual to find in private hands. The two dozen-odd S-76s registered in Australia are more typically employed in ferrying crews to offshore oil rigs and remote mine sites.

The Sikorsky is a sleek and handsome craft, with a wheeled undercarriage that retracts in flight. Packer's 1986-build example was nattily registered in 1999 as 'VH-CPH' (Consolidated Press Holdings). It's finished in frosted silver over a deep navy blue with a dark red stripe.

Wearing the same colour scheme, although more the helicopter equivalent of Sly Stallone in an Armani suit, is the Bell UH-1H Iroquois 205. The fabled 'Huey' of US and Australian military history, the stretched '205' specification is able to carry a 1500 kilogram payload and is configurable for up to 14 passengers or six stretchers. This example was built to US Army order in 1963, spending time with the US and later the German military. In 1999 it was 'civilianised' by US specialist, Garlick Helicopters, and sent to Australia.

In Packer's possession, the Huey flew only about 100 hours in ten years. It's now in the hands of Precision Helicopters, in Coffs Harbour, NSW, where it has flown several fire-fighting and flood-relief missions.

Christopher Lee, in *Howzat! Kerry Packer's War*, relates a story of Packer, John Cornell and an expectant Delvene Delaney being flown to a World Series Cricket game at VFL Park by helicopter. Packer, sitting up front in the (unnamed) chopper, asked the GTV9 Melbourne pilot Geoff Longland, 'Are these things as safe as light aircraft?'

Longland assured his boss that they were actually safer; that indeed, if the power were shut down to the main rotor, the blades would continue rotating and the chopper would just glide in to a landing.

'Okay,' Packer said. 'Turn the fuckin' thing off.' And against the voluble protestations of Cornell, the billionaire businessman and his nervous passengers made a voluntary noiseless landing at VFL Park.

Like Fitzgerald said: The rich are very different.

Part 3

FANTA & FINGER BUNS

'I'VE BEEN TO THE OTHER SIDE AND LET ME TELL YOU, THERE'S NOTHING THERE.'

Kerry Packer after his heart attack in 1990

'Son, there are two things that you're going to learn about me. One, that I'm hard to kill. And number two, I'm a gambler and I usually win.'

Kerry Packer to St Vincent's cardiologist Dr Ian Bailey, on their first meeting

10

THE HEALTH REPORT

The big dog in any fight usually has the advantage. And they didn't come much bigger, or fight much harder than Kerry Packer. At around 190 centimetres and 120 kilograms at the peak of his fitness, Packer was physically intimidating and he knew it. He once confessed, 'I don't know any other way to manage people, other than to scare the shit out of them.' He was a bloke who seemed bellicose and bulletproof.

In truth, Packer was enduring a rollercoaster ride of health issues that were as large and leveraged as the rest of his life. To the best of everyone's ability the details were always kept from the public record, not least for the reason that the physical status—and even the travel itineraries—of stratospheric CEOs like Packer can pressure the share values of their businesses.

It's been suggested that Packer's increasingly mercurial moods in the last years of his life were a by-product of the cocktails of medications he had to take just to stay alive.

In the weeks after Packer's death, James Packer gave some insight to the physiological time bomb that his father had been for a long time. 'There is no doubt that if you looked at the list of his ailments, they would have felled most people,' he said, on the documentary made by his father's Channel Nine. 'And there's no doubt that, at the age of 50, if someone had said to Dad, "You're going to live to 68" … It's too young, but I think from where he was at 50, most doctors would have said, no way.'

Kerry Packer had indeed been lucky to make it that far. At age seven, he fell victim to one of the waves of polio epidemics that swept Australia between 1930–50. The disease confined many children—including Packer—for months or even years at a time. Many were left with lifelong crippling injuries. From 1944, when Packer was stricken, to 1954, there were more than 17,000 cases notified and some 1000 deaths.

Packer spent nine months in an iron lung (actually, wooden ones were used in Australia), the pressure-machine helping his paralysed lungs to keep operating. Immobilisation of the patient was itself a critical part of the treatment, to avoid long-term damage to the spinal cord, nerves and muscles.

Those who came to know Packer later in life simply couldn't imagine this non-stop, insomniac, bull-at-a-gate individual in repose for such a length of time. 'I would think in a different age he'd have probably been diagnosed with ADHD or something like that,' says cricketer Greg Chappell, in all seriousness. 'He wasn't somebody who could sit still.'

The condition of dyslexia, the learning difficulty specific to reading and writing, had been known about since the late-19th century. But more widespread understanding of it would not come until the latter part of the 20th century. Packer was almost certainly dyslexic; later in life, reading would be one area that his formidable mental powers could not dominate. But in his early learning, further hindered by his medical isolation and subsequent relocation to Canberra, Packer himself seemed to have accepted his father's assessment of him as a 'boofhead'.

He bounced back physically, as he explained in his 1977 interview with journalist Terry Lane.

Long-time Nine personality Ray Martin told the story of a meeting with Packer, not long after the boss's 1990 heart attack. Martin was hoping for reassurance about his future at the network, and asked the man who'd taken back control of the station just 10 weeks before his heart stopped beating on the Warwick Farm polo field.

'Your future?' Packer retorted. 'Your fucking future? I don't know about *my* fucking future. Why should I give a rat's about *your* fucking future?'

The Bulletin, 4 January 2006

Ray Martin: You were dead for how long, Kerry?

KP: I don't know. Ten minutes? It's a bit hard to remember.

RM: Did you find anything out there?

KP: Do you want the good news or the bad news?

RM: Give us the good news.

KP: The good news is there's no Devil. The bad news is there's no Heaven.

RM: Is that right?

KP: Yeah. There's nothing.

Kerry Packer interviewed on *A Current Affair*, Nine Network, 16 February 1995

'Do you remember the time he died [but recovered]? He died at the weekend, on the Sunday. And it's Tuesday, and I wanted to get hold of Pat Wheatley—I figured she would be answering #10, which was Packer's number—she was #11—so I dialled #10.'

'[*in KP voice*]: "Yes?"'

'What the fuck are you doing there? You're supposed to be half dead!'

'He said, "I'm here doing my work. What are *you* doing?"'

TREVOR SYKES, FORMER EDITOR *THE BULLETIN*. (TWO DAYS AFTER KERRY'S DEATH 15 YEARS LATER, SON JAMES WOULD BE BACK AT HIS DESK FOR A FULL DAY'S WORK.)

'It was easier to look after 20 intensive care patients than one Kerry Packer.'

Dr Bob Wright at St Vincent's Hospital, quoted by Paul Barry in *The Rise and Rise of Kerry Packer*

'I was academically stupid and my way of surviving through school was sport. I used to play everything. I was never a great natural talent, but I worked hard at all the sports that I played and I became reasonably competent at all of them.'

At Geelong Grammar he acquitted himself more than adequately in a variety of sports and continued to spend enough time on the golf course that, in his early thirties, he played off a handicap of five.

In 1974, however, when at age 36 he inherited the multi-headed media business from his father, exercise and physical fitness began to take a back seat to the instant gratification of burgers, cream buns and lung-burners.

There were stories of Packer looking for instant fixes to his bad habits, investigating miracle diets and stop-smoking methods, including hypnosis. Around a decade and a half would pass before Australia's richest man began to comprehend that he could not simply pay someone to do what he would have to do for himself.

Packer's first major, publicised health scare in adulthood occurred in 1983, when he collapsed at The Australian golf course. It has been variously reported as an angina attack and a full-blown heart attack. He was taken to St Vincent's Hospital in Darlinghurst, in Sydney's inner-east, run by the Sisters of Charity.

For the Sisters, surgeons and staff, it would be the beginning of a long, often loud, challenging and wonderful relationship, the benefits of which would extend well beyond the parties directly involved.

In May 1986, Packer was again on the golf course, this time at Gleneagles in Scotland, when he collapsed and was rushed to hospital in London. There, he underwent operations for the removal of a cancerous kidney and diseased gall bladder. The urging of his doctors, plus the financial freedom provided by

Alan Bond less than 12 months later, prompted a Packer-sized embrace of polo.

For the next three years he trained quite hard, lost weight and made some more, fairly credible attempts to give up smoking.

Then, in October 1990, while playing for his Ellerston White team in the semi-finals of the Australian Open Polo Championship at Sydney's Warwick Farm racecourse, Packer suffered a massive heart attack that left him clinically dead for around seven minutes.

It's part of Packer legend that what was needed to save his life was a defibrillator; that only around 40 of NSW's 800-plus ambulances were equipped with one; and that one such ambulance, one of only 12 on duty for the entire Sydney metro area that day, happened to be driving past Warwick Farm during those critical few minutes.

Astonishingly, within three days of being dead, Packer was popping back into his Park Street office to keep an eye on the shop. The following weekend, he was back watching the polo. A week after that, Packer underwent bypass surgery, under Dr Victor Chang at St Vincent's.

KP was 53 years old—the same age his mother had been when she died of heart failure in New York, where she had flown for heart surgery at the Mayo Clinic. Kerry's grandfather, RC Packer, had been just one year older when he died in 1934, also of heart failure. Kerry's father, Sir Frank, had made it to 67 before heart failure and pneumonia claimed him.

KP had no obvious reason to be confident of a long life.

In September 1995, Packer suffered another suspected heart attack, collapsing at the Hakoah Club in Sydney. In July 1998, with his private McDonnell-Douglas DC-8 (a converted passenger jet) fitted out with medical equipment and staff, he flew to New York for another bout of bypass surgery.

It came in the middle of an Australian Broadcasting Authority enquiry into cross-media ownership. Arriving at the Cornell Medical Centre in New York, Packer checked in as 'James Fairfax, no fixed abode'. James Fairfax was the former chairman of the rival Fairfax publishing group.

'I lived [in Bowral] for two years, until one morning I got out of bed and just fell flat on my face. I had polio and rheumatic fever and I was sent straight down to Sydney.

'They put me in hospital there for about nine months, in an iron lung. When I got over that and made a good recovery, I was sent to Canberra, where the company had a place. The altitude was supposed to be the right thing for what I'd been through, so I was sent there with a nursing sister. I was lucky that my problem was diagnosed quickly and that I didn't try to strain myself, because I understand that's where the damage is done. But I couldn't walk and they thought I was trying to get out of school, because I loathed school.'

KERRY PACKER ON HIS CHILDHOOD IN *AS THE TWIG IS BENT*

'Do you understand what a major operation is? A major operation is what *you* have. And do you know what a minor operation is? That's the operation the bloke in the bed next door has. And that's the difference.'

Kerry Packer talking about his kidney transplant, *Australian Story*, ABC TV, 15 February 2001

'Imagine having a friend who is good enough to do that. For somebody to be generous enough to say: "Take it out of my body, you have a go." It was the most precious gift anyone could give you.'

Kerry Packer talking about his pilot, friend and kidney donor Nick Ross, *Australian Story*, ABC TV, 15 February 2001

Interviewer: 'The week prior I think you were in hospital and then the next day you were off to the States for surgery?'

KP: 'Well, that night I also had dinner with some politicians before I left, too ... operations don't worry me a lot. That may sound very strange to you, but I've had a lot of them and I believe I'm bulletproof. Therefore, the fact that I'm going to go and have an operation doesn't change my life at all.'

Kerry Packer being interviewed by the Australian Broadcasting Authority investigation into cross-media ownership, March 1999

'He hated hospitals and being constantly prodded by doctors ... there were times when he would just call for his car, tear off his monitors, tear off his oxygen drips and get up and walk out of a hospital when he had had enough.'

DR IAN BAILEY, PACKER'S CARDIOLOGIST, QUOTED BY ALAN JONES, *THE BULLETIN*, 4 JANUARY 2006

'I do not want to control Fairfax. Let me tell you why ... Last year I suffered a major heart attack and died. I didn't die for long, but it was long enough for me. I didn't come back to control John Fairfax.'

Kerry Packer to the 1991 print media enquiry into his shareholding in John Fairfax

The following year, Packer was in Sydney's Royal Prince Alfred Hospital having more surgery to clear his arteries. By now, despite other angioplasty surgeries to clear his kidney arteries, his remaining kidney was beginning to fail. His helicopter pilot and friend Nick Ross acknowledged, '[Packer] has had a rough bloody track medically all his life. Hasn't had a great deal of quality living in the last seven years. I wanted to help him, so I did.'

Ross' help was to donate one of his kidneys to his boss, a gesture that naturally touched Packer profoundly. The transplant was life-saving, but required ongoing therapy with anti-rejection drugs and steroids. One of the side-effects— were it miraculously not already present—was severe diabetes, which ignites another downward spiral.

Diabetes introduces a hardening of the arteries and associated heart problems. In 2002, some measure of how far medical technology had advanced lay in Packer's being implanted with a defibrillator. A dozen years earlier, Packer's whacker had arrived in a NSW Ambulance; this one was about the size of a matchbox. The unit had to be replaced after about 18 months, obviously in another surgical procedure.

In his last few years, Packer was often accompanied by a medical team equipped for any emergency. While he had shown a lifelong stoicism where medical matters were concerned, eventually the drugs, the hospitalisations, the gradual removal of the freedoms that made his life worth living, would culminate in a very logical decision to let the whole business wind down.

FANTA AND FINGER BUNS

Australians were always oddly fascinated by Kerry Packer's predilection for junk food. Here was Australia's wealthiest man, able to indulge a diet worthy of a James Bond villain, choosing instead to gorge on working-class grub.

For Packer, just possibly, it wasn't entirely a matter of choice.

He was not a man blessed with good health, and he very obviously had the willpower to achieve almost anything and the wherewithal to eat well. And yet, in the face of obesity, diabetes, heart and kidney problems and the unending advice of his doctors, Packer was strangely powerless to resist hamburgers, cakes, soft drinks and chocolate bars.

The same might also have been said of smoking and gambling, both of which were vigorously pursued and personally justified.

Alcohol often features on such lists, but Packer had eradicated it early from his life to become, with his idol Sir Don Bradman, one of the most famous teetotallers in Australia.

As with so many aspects of his life, Packer's abstinence from alcohol spawned a variety of myths and whispers. Packer himself, on *The Don Lane Show* in 1977, said 'Well, originally my father bribed me. He said, I will buy you a decent car when you're 21 if you don't drink and you don't smoke.'

Packer was equally dismissive of it in 2000 when, after his kidney transplant, he told ABC TV's *Australian Story*: 'I've got a face of a drinker, but the truth of the matter is I've always been a teetotaller.'

That wasn't quite the truth of it, as a subsequent, two-part *Australian Story* in 2014 revealed. It dug into the details of an horrific car crash in 1956 near Goulburn, NSW, in which the car Packer was driving collided head-on with another car. The three young men in the other vehicle were killed instantly. The 18-year-old Packer and his occupants—a mother and two children, family friends—escaped with injuries.

In giving details of the crash, the program interviewed former Packer friend Phillip Adams, who 'dimly' recalled KP

'I heard that he couldn't read. If he had somebody read everything to him, that would have taken a very long time. So I don't know about the dyslexia, I don't know if that's correct. But I do know that he was aware of everything that was ever printed in any of his publications, every week. Every word. You do not become a card player of his magnitude without having a phenomenally retentive memory. And that also meant that he remembered the by-lines of everyone who worked for him.'

PATRICK COOK, WRITER AND CARTOONIST

'He didn't read a lot. Everything we did would be one page, five bullet points. But he just used to spend huge amounts of time on the phone, just talking to people.'

Andrew Cowell, founding Art Director on *Cleo*

'He was pretty much dyslexic, and I showed him something one day – I forget what it was, some information about something – and he said, "You know better than to fuckin' show me. *Tell me.*" He knew where he was at with all that. Don't underestimate the power of the brain.'

Kevin Bartlett, racing driver and friend

'If I wanted Kerry to read something, I'd send him a short
didn't want him to read it, I'd send him a long memo! H
for his dyslexia by having a very good memory
advantage—and also by being very good at mer
got down there for one of his, what shall I call t
he was shooting the breeze and exploring idea
toes because he would be doing mental arith
"Well, if this happens and that happens, an
worth a million dollars over three years ..." A
yourself.'

TREVOR SYKES, FORMER EDITOR *T*

once telling him that this tragic event had marked the end of his drinking. Despite the sinister undertones, the accident had been thoroughly investigated at the time and the Coroner's report concluded that the vehicle carrying the three young men had been on the wrong side of the road. The Coroner cleared Packer of any blame.

However, the complete abstinence from drinking might suggest an inability to moderate; addictive tendencies, in other words. Packer once admitted as much to football coach and friend, Roy Masters. It's a template that certainly fits Packer's gambling, smoking—and his diet.

In general, Packer's favoured fat and sugar delivery systems were simply those from an earlier era, when popping out for some takeaway meant a two-fisted burger with the lot, a can of Fanta or Coke or Passiona, finally cemented in the stomach with a lamington or a caramel slice.

'[H]e was in the [*Women's Weekly*] office when the food trolley came around with food the Test Kitchen had made when they tested the recipes. He looked at the cakes and said, "Why doesn't that trolley come to my floor?" From that day on, it was always diverted to his office first.'

Ita Buttrose, *The Australian Women's Weekly*, February 2006

'**Kerry was a complex man,**' [actor Lachy] Hulme says. '**He smoked 80 cigarettes a day, had two quarter-pounders with cheese for lunch, maybe a couple more for dinner and he drank nothing but Fanta, or "freshly squeezed orange juice" as he called it. We didn't know that was his name for Fanta—(Nine chief) David Gyngell told us that and if we'd known that beautiful little bon mot, we would have whacked it into the script somewhere.**'

Actor Lachy Hulme, who played Kerry Packer in the Nine mini-series *Howzat!*, interviewed in *Adelaide Now*, 18 August 2012

'Mr P's favourite food was sponge cake with pink icing. Cathie Lonnie from the Test Kitchen went and cooked it at "The House" a few Christmases ago, and she made her mum's sponge cake (called Wendy's Sponge in our cookbooks). Mr P liked it so much, he had her teach his chefs how to make it and, while Cathie was there, she made a fresh one for him every day—with pink icing. Later, Mr P asked me to come up with a recipe for a fat-free finger bun (with pink icing, of course). He was very disappointed when I told him it would have to be eaten without butter. He probably liked the butter best. Mr P liked to call on the Test Kitchen for finger buns, grandchildren's birthday cakes, sponges and all.'

PAMELA CLARK, TEST KITCHEN DIRECTOR, *THE AUSTRALIAN WOMEN'S WEEKLY*, FEBRUARY 2006

'I remember going to a lunch there one day, I think it was in the [ACP] dining room – the whole fashion of that place was very 1970s, early 1980s. It was this big, important lunch, and there was a whole range of these top-of-the-town businessmen there, really important people who had been summoned to a meeting with Kerry. James was there, John Alexander, all the chiefs of PBL were there. And dessert was brought out, which was a platter of cheese, and a bowl of Violet Crumbles. As you do. Because Kerry loved Violet Crumbles.'

GARRY LINNELL, FORMER EDITOR OF *THE BULLETIN*

'He always used to stay at the Dorchester when he went over to London, until one day he came down, he just felt like a burger. Kerry's tastes were quite simple. On this particular day, all he wanted was a hamburger in the restaurant, and they tried to nick him for something like 20 quid for a hamburger—and this is 30 years ago. The rich will stand still for all sorts of things, but when they're being nicked on something small, they can really get indignant. And Kerry packed up that day and went to the Savoy. That's how the Savoy won him.'

TREVOR SYKES, FORMER EDITOR OF *THE BULLETIN*

'That day the Wig and Pen get-together after the case closed—drinks and a lavish afternoon tea—was like the dressing room after a good game, the mood buoyant, positive. Cornell says he approached Kerry and told him he'd just witnessed his finest innings ... He noticed Kerry wasn't listening, but standing there with a piggish look on his face. Cornell looked across and saw Lynton Taylor hovering over the splendid afternoon feast. At the close of the whole drama, "Kerry just wanted to finish talking and get to the cakes himself before Lynton ate them all."'

JOHN CORNELL OBSERVING PACKER'S PRIORITIES AFTER 31 OF GRUELLING DAYS OF HIGH COURT DRAMA IN LONDON, 1977. QUOTED IN *HOWZAT! KERRY PACKER'S WAR*

'I was talking to one of his doctors one day, we were talking about booze and what it does to you. He said, "When you have a drink, one of the things it does is relax the arterial walls – opens the arteries a bit. When you have a drag on a cigarette, that does the opposite, it closes them. So when you see Old Joe the barfly down at the end of the bar, having a fourpenny dark and a drag on a ciggie, he's actually keeping himself in some sort of balance." I said, "Christ, then we'd be better off if Kerry drank, rather than smoked." He said, "Well, yes – but I daren't suggest that to him."'

Trevor Sykes, former editor *The Bulletin*

. . . . ✦ . . . .

'I've always been a teetotaller, contrary to everybody's understanding. I mean, I've got a face of a drinker, but the truth of the matter is I've always been a teetotaller. Ah, and, you know, Nick doesn't look like a drinker, but he's got a drinker's kidney. I don't know that the kidney can handle much more milk, and ah, I don't know that I could handle the amount of scotch that it could handle. But I'm sure we'll come to some arrangement.'

Kerry Packer after his kidney transplant from helicopter pilot Nick Ross,
Australian Story, ABC TV, 15 February 2001

Kerry, a life-long non-drinker [*sic*], was there mixing happily with his players with the usual glass of Coke or Fanta or just water in his hand. At times like this the players often mischievously tried to get the Boss to join them in a beer. Kerry would politely decline. Kerry's non-drinking was at odds with his hard man, wharfie demeanour—it didn't quite fit the character.

CHRISTOPHER LEE, *HOWZAT! KERRY PACKER'S WAR*

'He didn't drink. But he didn't mind you having a drink in front of him. I think because he knew he could get more out of you if you were half-cut.'

Kevin Bartlett, racing driver and friend

[John] Singleton's last lunch with Packer was at Bondi Icebergs a couple of months ago. 'It went for seven and a half hours,' Singleton said. 'I set a world record for drinking mineral water ... He was too smart for me when I was sober. Imagine how far behind I'd be if I'd had 20 beers to his 20 mineral waters.'

'HOW HE CLINCHED A DEAL IN HIS DYING DAYS', ROY MASTERS, *SYDNEY MORNING HERALD*, 28 DECEMBER 2005

'I was always aware, I didn't think he was going to make old bones. We were conscious that we were planning for a post-Kerry era.'

Richard Walsh, *Australian Story*, ABC TV, 14 April 2014

'The Alan Bond deal was fantastic and he felt absolutely exhilarated, but unfortunately a few months later his health difficulties caught up with him and he suffered a massive heart attack on the polo field. He was in fact clinically dead for several minutes. But within days and with typical Packer bravado he was back on his feet and out at the polo field watching the polo. The fact that he survived gave it credence not to any sense that he was immortal, nor indestructible, but that he was, in the struggle between life and death, he was going to give a very good account of himself.'

RICHARD WALSH, *AUSTRALIAN STORY*, ABC TV, 14 APRIL 2014

'It takes me a fair while to unwind, I guess. I think the fact that I don't drink is one of the biggest drawbacks in my life. A couple of beers after work helps you unwind, but I can't do that. That's probably why I blow up every now and again.'

Kerry Packer quoted in Christopher Forsyth's *The Great Cricket Hijack*

'LIGHT MY CIGARETTE, SON.'

Kerry Packer to a 'prominent cardiologist', as reported
by Gideon Haigh in 'Packed It In: The Demise of
The Bulletin', *The Monthly*, March 2008

11

SMOKING OR FUMING

For a man with such formidable capacity to get things done, Kerry Packer struggled for much of his adult life with giving up the gaspers.

His suspected heart attack in 1983 prompted his first earnest attempts to stub out smoking. Packer recruited professional help from the Smokers Clinic at St Vincent's Hospital, Sydney and began buying cartons of the then-new nicotine chewing gum.

Neither the clinic nor the chewy got very far, but Packer was again attempting to abstain at the time of his 1990 heart attack on the Warwick Farm polo field. Packer survived seven minutes of death—and walked towards the lighter.

In 1996, Packer handed over a new BMW car to Sydney socialite Di Jagelman, after losing a bet over which of them would successfully quit first.

The evidence of one of the rare failures of Packer's iron will was to be seen in the photo taken of his desk on December 28 2005, two days after his death: an opened pack of Dunhill grey cigarettes, in an ashtray immediately to hand.

Packer was either chugging through cigs at the rate of 80 a day, or instructing his secretary Pat Wheatley to dole out a daily ration of just five. Among his executives, KP's state of nicotine numbing became a reliable barometer for the reception they could expect to receive.

'He was meant not to smoke and was constantly trying to give up. He was put on this regime by his secretary, Fairy [Maisie "Fairy" Faircloth] ... I think she was allowed to give him five cigarettes a day.

'I used to often see him in the morning and in the afternoon, when he used to come into the Art Department. He used to walk the floor quite a lot. He would come past my desk, sit down, pull a cigarette out of my packet—he never actually asked for one—but he always sat and smoked it with me.'

Andrew Cowell, founding art director of *Cleo*

'I have an addictive personality'

Kerry Packer to football coach and sports journalist, Roy Masters, quoted in *Sydney Morning Herald*, 28 December 2005

'You couldn't get within 20 feet of him without getting your head ripped off.'

— Kerry Packer's first and long-serving driver, George Young, observing the big man's mood during self-imposed smoking bans. Quoted in *The Rise and Rise of Kerry Packer*

'He paid $100,000 in advance, and Sylver went to the Mirage to hypnotise him. It worked. He stopped—for about 45 minutes.'

ON ONE OF HIS MANY GAMBLING TRIPS TO LAS VEGAS, PACKER PAID MAGICIAN AND HYPNOTIST MARSHALL SYLVER US$100,000 TO MAKE HIM STOP SMOKING. AS REPORTED BY AN ANONYMOUS SOURCE TO NORM CLARKE, *LAS VEGAS REVIEW JOURNAL*, 28 DECEMBER 2005

'There were times when I would hit some problem where I thought, the only fella around who can solve this is Kerry. And I never rang Kerry, I rang Pat [Wheatley] first up, who I knew quite well. I'd say, "Is he giving up smoking today?" And if she said, "No, no, he's smoking," I'd tentatively make an appointment. If she said, "Yes, he is," then I'd be going into a cavern with a bear with a sore head. And so I would try to fix the problem myself.'

Trevor Sykes, former editor *The Bulletin*

'He had the buzzer on the desk and had the secretary bring in a single cigarette every time he wanted a smoke. That was in the early 2000s, when he wasn't supposed to be smoking at all. There was the famous story about him telling the heart surgeon not to give him a fucking lecture. But I've been in there with him when he would hit the buzzer and Di or whoever was his PA at the time, would bring in one cigarette—just so he didn't have a packet sitting there.'

Garry Linnell, former editor of *The Bulletin*

'Around 1983, [Packer and Tony Greig] decided to quit smoking. This was a big deal. Kerry Packer did not drink alcohol; his drug was tobacco and he smoked as hard as he played, which was very hard indeed. His enthusiasm for his personal quit campaign was typically excessive. He converted old storerooms he owned in a building in Castlereagh St, Sydney, and built one of the city's plushest gyms, the Hyde Park Club. And there he and Greig began working out, staying off the fags for a whole nine months. Packer ordered his media executives to get fit, too, but it wasn't long before he became bored with the whole business.'

Tony Wright, *The Bulletin*, 4 January 2006

'I used to love staying up with Kerry in Ellerston and, you know, we'd smoke a thousand cigarettes, or we'd sit around on the floor and Kerry would wax lyrical about anything.'

Jodhi Meares, former daughter-in-law. *Australian Story*,
ABC TV, 14 April 2014

Part 4
LARGER THAN LIFE

'One thing you could say about Kerry was that if he was your friend, he was truly your friend ... he would do anything in the world for you and, in turn, you wanted to do anything for him.'

Jack Nicklaus, quoted by Alan Jones, 'Magic Moments',
The Bulletin, 4 January 2006

12

PICKING UP THE BILL

Stories about Kerry Packer dropping millions of dollars on business and gambling ventures aren't hard to find. Far less evident, however, are the stories of this billionaire helping out loyal employees who've fallen on hard times, or complete strangers in need, or hospitals and institutions whose services he would never conceivably use.

That's not because Packer never did any of this. He did plenty. But Kerry Packer losing $10 million on the tables at the Las Vegas Hilton or the London Ritz was something people wanted to read; Packer giving $30 million to cancer research, or $10 million to each of the Royal Prince Alfred Hospital and the Westmead Children's Hospital wasn't quite as newsworthy.

Packer strove as hard to keep secret his philanthropic giving as he did his gambling embarrassments.

Critics of the wealthy point out that, to someone of Packer's financial means, donating $10 million is equivalent to an average person donating $1000. Mathematically, that's true. And it's always enlightening to ask them: 'So, when did *you* last donate $1000 to charity?'

Packer's philanthropy seemed almost non-denominational. Quite aside from donating to medical institutions, he was known to—on a whim—fly a group of children to Disneyland, buy cars for unsuccessful quiz-show competitors, fund the preservation of a species and personally leap to the rescue of fallen friends.

'I'd watch him sitting at home at night looking at the telly and if someone failed to win a prize on a quiz, you know, and he was sort of touched by the story, he'd get on the hotline to the studio and demand that they be given a present. Now that was very much Kerry.'

PHILLIP ADAMS, *AUSTRALIAN STORY*, ABC TV, 7 APRIL 2014

During the Sydney debut of World Series Cricket, player David Hookes had his jaw smashed by a fast-rising ball. Packer instinctively took the situation into his own hands and raced the wounded sportsman in his Jaguar to St Vincent's Hospital in Darlinghurst.

Gerald Stone, writing in *Compulsive Viewing*, reflected on the actions of a man he would later come to know well. '[T]here was something in Kerry that reacted with visceral and immediate concern to hurt or discomfort in others. Those who knew him tell anecdotal tales of sudden and unexpected empathy coming from God knows where inside this big and brutal man.'

Stone goes on to suggest that this compassionate streak, which many saw extended to complete strangers, might be traceable to a childhood in which Packer experienced both sides of bullying.

Certainly, those who worked for him got to see these two sides—often within minutes of each other. 'Loyalty' is a word that cropped up often; respect was earned and returned.

In 1993, an ACP magazine editor was killed in a freak marine accident during a product launch event near Sydney. It was five days before Christmas. He left a wife and five young daughters. The editor had worked for Packer for no more than a few years, but he had been dedicated and was well-liked. In the days immediately after the accident Packer monitored the situation quietly but closely through the deceased man's staff and fellow editors.

A friend and colleague who was directly involved says Packer was concerned that the funeral be a fitting and appropriate send-off; he did not need to mention that he would pay for it. A day or two later, Packer called the colleague to his office and handed him a condolence card for the widow. The colleague later learned that it had contained a personal cheque for 'a substantial sum', believed to have constituted a few years' salary.

The colleague, to this day, is touched by the gesture—not for its scale, but for the sincerity he saw in KP.

That's the Kerry Packer they knew in Scone, NSW, the township 70 kilometres south-east of the Packers' Ellerston rural estate.

Sure, Packer most often travelled to Ellerston several thousand feet overhead, in his helicopter. But on the ground, the big bloke who got around in a flannelette shirt and moleskins or track-pants like everybody else, was well known for his random acts of kindness.

Packer donated televisions to the local hospital and was a supporter of the local Rural Fire Service. It was obviously prudent to be on the right side of both. But the scale of the Packers' presence and their policy of supporting local businesses whenever possible had a huge ripple effect.

There was one, unusual story concerning an order from Ellerston for a dozen or more leather sofas. They were supposedly destined for the private cinema on the property.

When they arrived at Ellerston, it was discovered that they were vinyl. Albeit, very good vinyl. Packer took matters into his own hands, phoning the retailer in high dudgeon.

'But Mister Packer,' the man protested, 'they're the highest-quality vinyl, most people can't tell the difference, and I realised I could save you a lot of money.' Packer checked the invoice and found that it was true.

He ordered the same quantity again, in leather. Paying for the lot, he instructed the man to donate the vinyl sofas to charity. A dozen hard-up local families got brand new sofas.

On a Monday afternoon in March 2001, four-year-old Amelia 'Millie' Qwast went missing from her family's homestead on the 39,000 hectare Glenrock Station property. There were fears that she may have fallen into the Schofields Creek, which runs through the property.

Glenrock Station is a neighbour to Ellerston, and when a full-scale search was mounted, around 100 Ellerston staff, including Packer's personal medical team and two Packer helicopters, were mobilised, joining local SES, police and the Westpac helicopter. Ellerston also sent food and refreshments out to the searchers.

Many people never knew what Kerry Packer did, but Kerry Packer thought a great deal about, and for, other people. I don't know that anybody comes close to Kerry Packer in the area of concern and generosity."

BROADCASTER JOHN LAWS

'When he gave me my heart operation, he wouldn't let me pay for it, so he got square with me at a later date.'

Kerry Packer speaking at the launch of the Victor Chang Cardiac Research Institute in February 1994

'I don't know what to say about Victor, except that when I heard Victor had been shot, I cried, and I don't cry often. He was an extraordinary man, and he was a man that, when he left, the world missed him. Many of us when we go, we're not going to be missed. Victor was.'

Kerry Packer speaking at the launch of the Victor Chang Cardiac Research Institute in February 1994

'I'd been [with *The Bulletin*] just on 18 years, but I was a contributor. That meant they didn't owe me anything. I became extremely ill in 2005 with a brain tumour, and Mr Packer, possibly prompted by others who knew, he kept my family on the cheque, through a very ordinary year. My weekly contributor's payment kept coming in, while I wasn't capable of contributing anything ... the operation had given me a stroke as well, I was in a wheelchair in Sacred Heart. I was out of action for at least nine months, tried to go back to work and was useless ...

'I'm just continually grateful to him. It was such a good thing to have done. I'm sure it would have taken about three words. Somebody would have said, "Such-and-such is really crook." "What's wrong with him?" They would have told him, and then somebody would have pointed out that I was a contributor and they weren't obliged to pay me. "Pay 'im." I don't know. But I hope he considered me a loyal person, which I was.

'I feel I'm one small example of a very large line-up of people to whom he was generous—prompted or unprompted. But he never asked for thanks, or as far as I know, made a mention of it. He knew, and the recipient knew.'

Patrick Cook, writer and cartoonist for *The Bulletin*

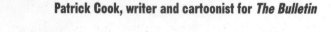

'He certainly looked after people who had been there for a long period of time. You heard lots of stories about him paying off mortgages, picking up people's medical expenses—but you used to hear them as gossip, "Kerry looked after such-and-such"... I know he had owned lots of properties, especially in Woollahra, and it's gossip—but people on hard times, he used to let them use his houses. So I was told ... I just know that that stuff happened, it was never really talked about.'

ANDREW COWELL, FOUNDING ART DIRECTOR ON *CLEO* AND LATER CREATIVE DIRECTOR AT ACP

Thankfully, Millie was found in good health the following afternoon, 24 hours after the crisis had begun. She was eight kilometres from the homestead and, on realising she was lost, had curled up next to her dog, Dasha, and slept for the night.

Millie's mother, writer Andrea Qwast, told *The Sydney Morning Herald* in 2005, 'He [Packer] was an amazing man. He just dropped everything, just to look for our little girl.'

One who regularly saw this very caring side of Packer, and was witness to much of his unreported generosity, was Sister Anthea Groves, the patient liaison officer of St Vincent's Hospital, Sydney. Sister Anthea was mentored by the almost-sainted Sister Bernice (Sister Mary Bernice Elphick), who died in 2008.

Packer's largesse would extend to many hospitals, and late in his life he would entrust himself to Royal Prince Alfred in Sydney's Inner West, where his father Sir Frank had spent his final days. But there was a sentimental attachment to St Vincent's: Kerry's grandfather, Herbert Henry Bullmore, had been a leading physician there from 1911 until his death in December 1937, when Kerry was 11 days old.

Sister Anthea, who completed her nursing training at St Vincent's in 1960, worked with Kerry and Ros Packer on several fundraising projects. Among them was the 2004 launch of the David Hookes Foundation, raising awareness of organ donation after Hookes' death.

In 1977, Hookes had been brought to the same building after that terrifying ride in the Packer Jag. Sister Anthea smiles as she recalls Packer's actions. 'Well, see, that's Kerry—the spontaneous part of Kerry. And I think that's why he was a lovable larrikin, in a way. He did care for people.'

Sister Anthea's predecessor, Sister Bernice, managed the hospital from 1963 to 1997. Sister Bernice had a robustly entrepreneurial approach and drove the expansion of the hospital's private and medical research facilities. Packer once described her as 'the greatest fundraiser of all time.'

There was, Sister Anthea says, no end of respect between the apparently flint-hard businessman and the selfless, but no less persuasive Sister of Charity. "You might say she wheeled and dealed a bit, but it was always in the cause of our mission."

Among the publicly-known examples of Packer's slings to St Vincent's were, in the aftermath of his first bout of heart trouble in 1983, the outfitting of the Intensive Care ward with new cardiac monitoring equipment.

According to Paul Barry's telling in *The Rise and Rise of Kerry Packer*, the Big Fella insisted on personally doing that 1983 deal from his bedside with supplier Hewlett Packard, telling its boss: 'I've never paid the full price for anything in my life. Now, where's the quote?'

A no less significant memento of that era was the provision of Packer's Falcon 200 private jet to be on permanent standby for the collection of human organs anywhere in Australia or New Zealand. That is to say: every recipient of a transplant at St Vincent's, Sydney from 1984 to Packer's death in 2005—and beyond, under James Packer—has had their organs delivered courtesy of the Packer family.

In 1993, Packer picked up the bill for a lithotripter, a machine that transformed the treatment of kidney stones from a four-day hospital stay to a 45-minute treatment without need of anaesthetic.

'They did the lithotripsy,' recalls Sister Anthea, 'and he said, "How much, sister?"' She said, 'Three million, Mr Packer'— she always called him Mr Packer when they were doing business. And the cheque came out.

Packer's most publicised visit to St Vincent's was after his 1990 heart attack on the polo field, where he had been dead for seven or eight minutes. His surgeon, Dr Bob Wright, explained to the still bedridden Packer how lucky he had been that an ambulance nearby had been one of the few in Sydney equipped with a defibrillator machine.

Radio commentator Alan Jones described Mr Packer as a 'quiet giver', who was 'phenomenally generous'. He recalled having just started at Sydney radio station 2UE and taking a call from a listener who was planning an upcoming wedding. The man was planning to surprise his wife with a new Holden car but it was stolen.

'One of the girls came in and they said, "I think Kerry Packer's on the line ..."' Mr Jones told Macquarie Radio. 'He said, "Son, just tell that fella I'll fix it up as long as no-one knows."'

'PACKER LEGACY TO LIVE ON THROUGH CHARITY', *AAP*, 27 DECEMBER 2005

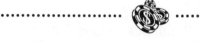

'The Packer Theatre at Ascham—he was devastated, he really tried hard for it not to be called the Packer Theatre. He really didn't want that.'

Andrew Cowell, on the 700-seat theatre built at a Sydney girls' private school, from a $1 million donation by Kerry Packer. The theatre is the subject of a popular story that Packer's daughter Gretel was to be expelled, and that Kerry Packer asked headmistress Rowena Danziger, 'Okay, what's it going to cost me?' It's a great story—and there's a very similar one about Cranbrook boys' school benefitting from Sir Frank when a young Kerry thumped a sports master—but Danziger has denied it.

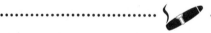

'Who could guess that on some nights Kerry hovers like a guardian angel? If a particularly worthy contestant—perhaps a battler with a heart-wrenching hard-luck story to tell—just misses out, he's on the phone to order an instant reversal of the decision.

'"What a wonderful woman. Give her the car! Give her the car! I'll pay for it!" Which he does, on three or four occasions. His spontaneous reaction is exactly what most people watching from their homes are feeling at the time—give her the car, give her the car—except this sympathetic viewer happens to own the network.'

GERALD STONE, *COMPULSIVE VIEWING*

'Last year, [A Current Affair] told of the plight of a little girl who needed an operation—costing $136,000. Kerry was quickly on the phone, saying, "I'll pay for it. But say nothing."'

Ray Martin, *The Bulletin*, 4 January 2006

'He did often mention how lucky he was to be able to get the sort of treatment he did. But he also felt sorry for other people that didn't have the sort of care that we could deliver. He certainly cared for people at all levels. ... I can only say there are certainly a lot of people walking around alive today because of something he did.'

Paramedic Paul Featherstone, veteran of the Granville train disaster and Thredbo landslide, who flew with Packer for his 1998 heart surgery in New York and became a friend. 'Packer legacy beats on in hearts and minds', *Sydney Morning Herald*, 31 December 2005

'I went one day to the Sydney Football Stadium with Kerry Packer, before they put boxes in. And we had to go and find our own seats in the Members section. We found our four seats, and we then decided we were hungry and wanted to have something to eat, so we went inside. Just as we went, Kerry said to this little kid, who was sitting in a wheelchair behind us, "Can you see to it that no-one takes these four seats?" So, this little guy could hardly speak, but he nodded and said, "Yeah." We went and had our meal and we watched through the window. This little guy wouldn't let anyone go anywhere near those seats. We watched the rugby, at the end of the rugby Kerry said to the guardian of this little boy, "Right. These five mates, plus five others, and all their parents—give me a call tomorrow in the office. I want them all, on me, to go to Disneyland." I mean, those little things he did all the time.'

TONY GREIG, *BIG FELLA: THE EXTRAORDINARY LIFE OF KERRY PACKER*, NINE NETWORK, 16 FEBRUARY 2006

Packer, no stranger to the whim of Lady Luck, called NSW Premier Nick Greiner on the spot and relayed Dr Wright's estimate that equipping all 888 of the ambulances in NSW with a defibrillator would cost $5 million. Packer famously said: 'I'll go you halves.'

The ambulance fit-out, launched in February 1991, would become the world's largest early-defibrillation program. And the diction-challenging machines would enter Aussie argot as 'Packer whackers'.

After Packer's subsequent triple-bypass operation in late-October 1990, a friendship was forged with the brilliant heart surgeon, Dr Victor Chang. It would be tragically cut short just nine months later, when Chang was murdered during an attempted extortion.

Chang's research and his memory would be perpetuated in the Dr Victor Chang Cardiac Research Institute, founded in 1994 with a donation of $3 million from Packer and $3 million from the federal government.

Somewhat more bizarrely, archivist Anne Cooke notes another Packer donation towards the Institute: that of a 750 kilograms, two-year-old Brahman bull named 'Buster', from Packer's Newcastle Waters station in the Northern Territory. The occasion was a 1994 fundraising auction in Darwin.

It's not likely that the animal ultimately benefitted from that transaction, but sometimes they did. In the late 1970s, Packer was a member of the board on the Western Plains Zoo, then being developed in the central NSW town of Dubbo. The zoo's black rhino breeding program was beset with delays and faced almost certain abandonment. Packer, having already donated considerable sums to the zoo, stepped up again and saved the program.

In 2000, Packer received a kidney from his pilot and friend, Nick Ross. The operation was done at Royal Prince Alfred Hospital. In the wake of that, Packer gifted $10 million to the hospital—the largest donation in its history—with which it constructed a new training facility, and rebuilt its renal transplant unit. At Packer's suggestion, the refurbished kidney clinic was subsequently renamed the Nick Ross Clinic. Packer was reportedly less excited about the education centre carrying his name.

Indeed, it's among few institutions to carry the name of this enormous benefactor. (The $80 million Packer-Lowy Institute at St Vincent's, headquarters of the Victor Chang Cardiac Research Institute and other research bodies, was a 2008 initiative of respective family scions, James and Steven).

Those carrying Kerry's name include the Kerry Packer Theatre at Ascham, the exclusive Sydney eastern suburbs girls' school which Packer's mother and daughter had both attended. On the other side of town, serving Sydney's working-class west there is the Kerry Packer Institute for Child Health Research at Westmead Hospital. It arose from a donation of $10 million from Packer, backed by his challenge to state and federal governments to each match his gift.

Perhaps the greatest legacy has been that wife Ros and children James and Gretel have not only perpetuated, but very possibly surpassed, the culture of charitable giving that Kerry started.

'I have never forgotten, it must have been 15 years ago, I was on an aircraft, or 20 years ago, travelling to America and I got a note to see some people, they were in the middle of the plane. I wandered down to talk to them and I came across a group of people who were going across to Disneyland, and they were obviously from disadvantaged circumstances and I deduced from something that somebody said that [Packer] had been responsible for it. Now, that is just a random example of the sort of generosity...'

FORMER PRIME MINISTER JOHN HOWARD, MEDIA CONFERENCE IN SYDNEY AFTER PACKER'S DEATH, 27 DECEMBER 2005

'He couldn't sit at home and listen to a telethon for a children's hospital without jumping on the phone and contributing. I don't know whether it was ever identified, but he had a spontaneity about him for a good cause—and sick kids were a good cause, so far as he was concerned.'

Sister Anthea Groves, St Vincent's Hospital

'He says it has been a great joy to know her—but that it has not been inexpensive.'

Ros Packer, when asked Kerry Packer's opinion of Sister Bernice Elphick. 'The one woman in the world Kerry can't say no to', *The Sun-Herald*, 18 April 2004

'There are only two
people I trust to
manage my estate,
and that's you and
Lloyd Williams. I
am going with Lloyd
because you drink
too much.'

KERRY PACKER, NOT LONG BEFORE HE DIED, TO JOHN SINGLETON.
QUOTED IN 'THE FRIENDS AND FOES OF JOHN SINGLETON',
THE SUNDAY TELEGRAPH, 5 MAY 2013

13

ON DEADLINE

The end for Kerry Francis Bullmore Packer came at 10.40pm on Boxing Day, 2005. For months he had looked ill. Several people had described his skin as looking like rice paper. He was regularly accompanied by a medical attendant. But in many ways, the Packer planets were revolving as usual.

In late October, Kerry had been in Argentina to watch his thrice-champion Ellerstina team compete in the Argentine Open polo, which it lost narrowly to rising team La Dolfino. Packer was said to have travelled with a full medical staff.

He returned to Australia not long before Christmas, putting together a brazen $780 million pitch for five years of television rights for the AFL. It was typically Packer: a win-it-or-bin-it offer which, even if it should fail, would seriously hobble the rival Seven/Ten bid. Packer signed the bid in his Park Street office on 22 December and it was accepted by the AFL on 23 December.

Packer had just three more days to live.

It seems likely that it was on 22 December that Packer made a special phone call to his son, James.

Perhaps only Kerry Packer knew what he had planned, though there had been no shortage of hints. Or of practice runs: Lloyd Williams, the close Packer confidant who was ultimately executor of Kerry Packer's estate, told the *Sydney Morning Herald* in 2013 that he had been summoned to Packer's presumed deathbed three times in the final four years.

'I don't want
to hang around
when there's no
hope. Do you?
I don't want to
lose my dignity.
Don't want people
fussing about me
and telling me
when I want to
take a leak and
all that. Couldn't
think of anything
worse. Could you?'

Kerry Packer as quoted by Les Carlyon, 'A giant among men', *The Bulletin*,
4 January 2006

ON DEADLINE

But this time was different. 'Kerry knew he was going to die four or five days before the event,' Williams said. 'All his organs were failing.'

Packer had told his doctors not to prolong his life. He was a very sick man, but he was even sicker of the dialysis, of the increasing indignity that remaining alive entailed. It was said that he had not been living at home for the last few years of his life—but he wanted to die there, not hooked up to yet another machine, in yet another hospital.

James was spending his Christmas aboard *Arctic P* in the Maldives, in the north Indian Ocean, when he received the phone call from his father. It was, James later said, an hour-long call that was very gentle and revealing. He would better understand its significance 24 hours later when a doctor phoned, urging him to return home immediately.

All the wealth in the world cannot shrink the size of the planet. With the *Arctic P* somewhere among the 1200 islands of the Maldives, James' best-case scenario for getting home would have a helicopter landing on the deck and rushing him to the Ibrahim Nasir airport on Hulhule Island, where the family's Falcon 200 private jet would be awaiting takeoff to Sydney, at least three fuel stops notwithstanding.

Perhaps commercial flights, for all the emotional turmoil that James must have been feeling, would get him home faster. Author Gerald Stone reported that James flew home commercially, changing flights in Singapore, and finally arriving at the Bellevue Hill home at 9pm on Boxing Day.

Kerry Packer died at 10:40pm.

Kerry's grandfather, RC Packer, and his parents, Sir Frank and Lady Gretel Packer, are all interred in the Packer family tomb at Sydney's South Head Cemetery. Kerry, however, had wanted to be buried on his beloved Ellerston estate. Being private property, the family had to secure the council's consent.

The funeral service was intensely private, attended only by wife Ros, and James and Gretel with their respective partners.

It was quite a contrast to the media frenzy, VIP roll-out and slick, Nine Network-quality production of the State Memorial

Service held for him several weeks later at the Sydney Opera House.

On 27 December 2011, six years and one day after Kerry Packer died, an extraordinary cargo was due to arrive on Australian soil. Artemis, a nine-metre tall, four-tonne bronze statue of a horse's head, was cast in 2010 by British artist Nic Fiddian-Green. After standing for just over a year at the historic Goodwood racecourse in West Sussex, not far from Packer's UK estate, it had journeyed from England via the Panama Canal.

The sculpture, it was said, had been bought by the widow of an Australian media mogul 'with strong links to the equine world' and would become a memorial at his graveside. Renamed by the artist as *I Look Beyond for a Distant Land*, there can have been no more fitting—or fittingly large—monument to Kerry Packer.

The famous phone calls had become less frequent as Packer's health declined and Sam Chisholm returned to run [Channel Nine] his way. A producer, in a moment of madness, said to Packer: 'I miss your phone calls—I miss the rockets.'

'I'm too tired, son,' came the reply.

Steve Crawley, *The Bulletin*, 4 January 2006

'One of the true joys of my life is that my father and I ended in a, um, in a perfect spot ... My last conversation with my father was a sort of, was an amazing, was an amazing experience as I look back on it. And I didn't realise it was going to be my last conversation with him. It was at the end of 2005 and dad had been sick for probably 10–15 years before that, and on many occasions we had spoken about the fact that he thought he could be in real trouble and he could be about to die, and had those conversations. And at the end of 2005 he wasn't well, but there was not a sense that he was about to die.

'I was on holidays, it was Christmas time and the phone rang and I was overseas, 24 hours from Sydney and it was Dad. And I wasn't expecting a call and I always got the bit jumpy when Dad called—I didn't know if it was going to be a good call or a bad call—and it was a beautiful call, for about an hour. And it was a strange call, and I look back on now and obviously understand what it was.

'He said he loved me, he said he was proud of me and he said ... that he wanted me to know that, you know, if anything ever happened to him, he wanted me to live my life my way and never think about what he would have done, or what would he want me to do. So it was a strange call, and anyway, it was a lovely call.

'Put down the phone, and 24 hours later his doctor rang and said, "Get on the plane, he's got 24 hours to live." And I got home and held his hand and he passed. Dad knew and he didn't tell me. He was a fucking big man, Mike, he was the big man. Pretty cool, pretty cool.'

JAMES PACKER TO MIKE WILLESEE, *SUNDAY NIGHT*, CHANNEL 7, 10 FEBRUARY 2013

'I spoke with him just before Christmas. He somehow knew his time was up and he said to me: "I can't eat what I want to eat, drink what I want to drink, do what I want to do or go where I want to go. Son, what is the point of it?"

'Normally you would gee him up, but on this occasion, I think I said something fairly useless like: "Whatever, champion, we will be with you."'

ALAN JONES, 'MAGIC MOMENTS', *THE BULLETIN*, 4 JANUARY 2006

'I saw him just a couple of days before he died. I was stunned by how weak he was, he was very thin. And he'd decided he wouldn't get any treatment. There'd be no dialysis. He'd just go.'

Graham Richardson, *Australian Story*, ABC TV, 14 April 2014

'I was home, on holidays, and Ros rang me in the morning. On Boxing Day. I'd known that he wasn't well and that James had come home. I was very sad. But she told me the arrangements, that it was going to be private. She, I suppose ... she worried about his afterlife. She could discuss that with me. I would understand that. And I said "Ros, by his good works ... [glances upwards] he won't be knocked back." And it's true of all people. You go through life, you find people who never get near a church or believe in the church or whatever, but if they're really good people ... I don't fear the Fella upstairs. I don't think anyone should.'

Sister Anthea Groves, St Vincent's Hospital

'As a child, I didn't think my life was at all unusual. Some people might be surprised to hear it, but we had a very normal childhood. We were a close family. We went to school, had to do our homework, the dogs slept on the beds and we played with our father in the swimming pool. As I grew older, I realised what an incredible gift Dad was. He may not have been tame and he was rarely predictable, but he was out of the ordinary—unique. He was one of the funniest people I have ever known. He had an extraordinary dry wit and great comic timing. I feel blessed to have had him as my father.'

Gretel Packer, *The Australian Women's Weekly*, February 2006

'Kerry was a stunningly brilliant media operator. He was charming and irreverent and great company. He was a dedicated patriot who helped make Australia an exciting place to live in. For that alone he should be mourned, even by his enemies.'

RICHARD WALSH, 'SHREWD OPERATOR', *THE BULLETIN*, 4 JANUARY 2006

'My God, I've never met a more powerful bloke, a silverback gorilla, the apotheosis of masculinity, courageous and frightening, funny and charming, clever and witty and world-weary—just a wonderful bunch of things. He was extraordinary, I was dazzled.'

Posie Graeme-Evans, on being interviewed in Packer's Park St dining room for the prized spot as head of drama at Nine. In *Compulsive Viewing*

'I wonder just how long it will take many other Australians to realise what they've lost—an outstanding philanthropist, the savviest businessman I've ever met and, underlying it all, a decent human being. We used to talk sometimes about the tall poppy syndrome in this country.'

GREG NORMAN, *THE BULLETIN*, 4 JANUARY 2006

'It is a very big loss for Australia, because he was a passionate believer in this country. I was always struck when I spoke to him that he was full of ideas about what should be done to make this a better country, and that was something that always made him a very attractive person. Sure he was an influential businessman, he believed in looking after his own interests. He made no apologies for doing that. He wouldn't want to have been thought doing otherwise. But always there was a concern about Australia and he was a passionate believer in this country's decency and worth and always wanting to do something to better it.'

FORMER PRIME MINISTER JOHN HOWARD, MEDIA CONFERENCE AT KIRRIBILLI HOUSE,
27 DECEMBER 2005

'There are so many things about Kerry that were fascinating but he … just his presence, just his existence. Like, he was just such a big being, you know, he took up a lot of space. He was just there, you know, and he came with a force.'

Jodhi Packer, first wife of James Packer,
Australian Story, ABC TV, 7 April 2014

'He had his faults, he had big faults, but that's just nothing compared to the fact that he was a very dynamic man. Whatever critique I might have of him as a person doesn't touch the sides of the fact that he did achieve a lot.'

RICHARD WALSH, FORMER PUBLISHER AT ACP, _AUSTRALIAN STORY_, ABC TV, 14 APRIL 2014

'The innings was too short, but there were a lot of runs.'

Alan Jones, at Packer's memorial service, 17 February 2006

REFERENCES

BOOKS

Barry, P. (1993). *The rise and rise of Kerry Packer.* Milsons Point, NSW: Bantam.

Buttrose, I. (1985). *Early edition: my first forty years.* South Melbourne, Vic: Macmillan.

Callander, K. (2009). *Good luck and good punting.* Sydney, NSW: Pan Macmillan.

Castleman, D. (2004). *Whale hunt in the desert: the secret Las Vegas of superhost Steve Cyr.* Las Vegas, USA: Huntington Press.

Chenoweth, N. (2006). *Packer's lunch: a rollicking tale of Swiss bank accounts and money-making adventures in the roaring '90s.* Crows Nest, NSW: Allen & Unwin.

Dunlap, A. J. (1997). *Mean business: how I save bad companies and make good companies great.* New York: Simon & Schuster.

Forsyth, C. (1978). *The great cricket hijack.* Camberwell, Vic: Widescope.

Lane, T. (1979). *As the twig is bent.* Melbourne, Vic: Dove Communications.

Latham, M. (2005). *The Latham Diaries.* Carlton, Vic: Melbourne University Publishing.

Lee, C. (2012). *Howzat!: Kerry Packer's war.* Sydney, NSW: NewSouth Publishing.

Sailor, W. (2013). *Wendell Sailor: crossing the line.* Cammeray, NSW: Simon and Schuster.

Stone, G. (2000). *Compulsive viewing: the inside story of Packer's Nine Network.* Ringwood, Vic: Viking.

Stone, G. (2007). *Who killed Channel 9?: the death of Kerry Packer's mighty TV dream machine.* Sydney, NSW: Pan Macmillan Australia.

Wilkins, R. (2012). *Black ties, red carpets, green rooms*. Chatswood, NSW: New Holland.

TELEVISION

ABC. (1979). Kerry Packer [Television series episode]. In *Parkinson in Australia*. Sydney, NSW: Australian Broadcasting Corporation.

ABC. (1991, September 16). Warren Anderson [Television series episode]. In *Four Corners*. Sydney, NSW: Australian Broadcasting Corporation.

ABC. (2001, February 14). Best of friends. In *Australian Story*. Sydney, NSW: Australian Broadcasting Corporation.

ABC. (2004, April 15). George meets Ita [Television series episode]. In *George Negus tonight*. Sydney, NSW: Australian Broadcasting Corporation.

ABC. (2011, August 15). Ita tells me so – part 1. In *Australian Story*. Sydney, NSW: Australian Broadcasting Corporation.

ABC. (2014, April 14). A complicated life: Kerry Packer – part 2. In *Australian Story*. Sydney, NSW: Australian Broadcasting Corporation.

ABC. (2014, April 7). A complicated life: Kerry Packer – part 1. In *Australian Story*. Sydney, NSW: Australian Broadcasting Corporation.

Channel Nine. (1991, November **) Kerry Packer [Television series episode]. In *A Current Affair*. Sydney, NSW: Nine Network.

Channel Nine. (1995, February 16). Kerry Packer [Television series episode]. In *A Current Affair*. Sydney, NSW: Nine Network.

Channel Nine. (2006, February 16). *The big fella: the extraordinary life of Kerry Packer*. Sydney, NSW: Nine Network.

Channel Seven. (2012, September 20). Sir David Frost [Television series episode]. In *Sunday Night*. Sydney, NSW: Channel Seven.

Channel Seven. (2013, 10 February). James Packer [Television series episode]. In *Sunday Night*. Sydney, NSW: Channel Seven.

Denton, A. (2003, 5 May). Episode 8 – Rene Rivkin [Television series episode]. In *Enough Rope*. Sydney, NSW: Australian Broadcasting Corporation.

RADIO

Epstein, R. (Presenter). (2004, September, 30). Interview with Steve Cyr. In *Drive* [Radio broadcast]. 774 ABC Melbourne.

Trembath, B. (Presenter). (2006, February 17). Interview with Dr Bridget Griffen-Foly. In *The World Today* [Radio broadcast]. ABC Radio National.

Trembath, B. (Presenter). (2006, February 17). Interview with Ray Martin. In *The World Today* [Radio broadcast]. ABC Radio National.

Trioli, V. (Presenter). (2006, February 17). Interview with Peter Costello. In *Kerry Packer Memorial Service* [Radio broadcast]. 702 ABC Radio.

SPEECHES AND MEDIA STATEMENTS

Beazley, K. (2005, December 27). Media statement on Kerry Packer's death.

Benaud, R. (2006, February 17). Speech at Kerry Packer's memorial service. Sydney Opera House, NSW.

Howard, J. (2005, December 27). Press conference on Kerry Packer's death at Kirribilli House, Sydney, NSW.

Jones, A. (2006, February 17). Speech at Kerry Packer's memorial service. Sydney Opera House, NSW.

Laws, J. (2005). Statement to media on Kerry Packer's death.

Martin, R. (2008). *Andrew Olle Media Lecture.* Sydney, NSW: Australian Broadcasting Corporation.

Merriman, B. (2005, May). Speech for Cricket Australia's Centenary.

Murdoch, R. (2005). Statement to the media on Kerry Packer's death.

Packer, J. (2006, December 26). Speech for anniversary of Kerry Packer's death and announcement of Kerry Packer Foundation. Melbourne Cricket Ground, Vic.

Packer, J. (2006, February 17). Speech at Kerry Packer's State memorial service. Sydney Opera House, NSW.

Packer, R. (2007, January 30). Speech at the sesquicentenary of St Vincent's Hospital. Sydney, NSW.

GOVERNMENT REPORTS

Australian Broadcasting Authority. (1999). *Investigation into control: Mr Brian Powers, Mr Kerry Packer and Mr James Packer/ John Fairfax Holdings Limited.* March 1999. Sydney, NSW: Australian Broadcasting Authority.

Cth. House of Representatives. (2000, August 31). Statements by Members. Mark Latham, MP. Pg. 19912.

House of Representatives. (1991). *Kerry Packer's appearance at the Select Committee on Print Media.* Canberra, ACT: Sound and Vision Office, Parliament of Australia.

NEWSPAPERS AND MAGAZINES

A Tribute to Kerry Packer. (2006, February). *The Australian Women's Weekly.*

Bartley, P. (2008, October 28). Bookie recalls millions of reasons Packer were racing. *The Age.*

Blake, M. (2005, December 28). Sporting life. *The Age.*

Bourke, T. (2005, December 30). The big fella and the power of the punt. *The Age.*

Braithwaite, D. (2006, February 17). Kerry's send off turns rough. *The Sydney Morning Herald.*

Business Review Weekly Rich List. (1999, May 28). *Business Review Weekly.*

Chappell, I. (2012, August 19). Kerry Packer's cricket revolution changed the way the game was played forever. *Daily Telegraph.*

Clark, Norm (2005, December 28). *LasVegas Review Journal.*

Crabb, A. (2009). *Stop at nothing: the life and adventures of Malcolm Turnbull.* Quarterly Essay 34, June. Collingwood, Vic: Black Inc.

Craddock, R. (2013, May 2). John Singleton, man of the people, always stays true to his words. *The Courier-Mail.*

Curro, T. (2006). A fortunate life. *Australian Women's Weekly, February,* 38.

Davis, S. (2000, August 31). Gambler Packer loses £13 million in 3 days. *The Telegraph.*

Gibbs, S. (2005, December 31). Packer legacy beats on in hearts and minds. *The Sydney Morning Herald.*

Greig, T. (2006, February). 'My friend Kerry'. *The Wisden Cricketer.*

Haigh, G. (2008, March). 'Packed it in: the demise of The Bulletin'. *The Monthly.*

Haselhurst, D. (2008, October 30). Packer's Miss Moneypenny. *The Age.*

Kaplan, M. (2006, March/April). 'Remembering the world's greatest gambler'. *Cigar Aficionado*

Kerry Packer. (2013, September 12). bet-like-a-pro.com. Retrieved from http://www..bet-like-a-pro.com/gamblers/kerry-packer

Kerry Packer was last of a breed. (2006, January 3). *Gaming Today Online.* Retrieved from http://www.gamingtoday.com

Lampe, A. (2005, December 7). James blank on father's sickbed meeting. *The Sydney Morning Herald.*

Mallett, A. (2011, December 25). *What Kerry did.* ESPN Cricinfo Magazine. Retrieved from http://www.espncricinfo.com/magazine/content/story/546174.html

Masters, R. (2005, December 28). How he clinched a deal in his dying days. *The Sydney Morning Herald*.

Norrie, J. (2005, December 29). 'I think I'll have two doctors on rye'. *The Age*.

Packer blows $60 million in Vegas. (2001, September, 26). *AAP*.

Packer legacy to live on through charity. (2005, December, 27). *AAP*.

Packer loses $20 million' at cards. (2000, August 31). *BBC News Online*. http://news.bbc.co.uk

Packer, R. (2008). Life after Kerry. *Australian Women's Weekly, October*, 47-48.

Pomerantz. D. (2014). James Packer's next big gamble is on Hollywood. *Forbes*, 24 March.

Pougher, D. (2012, August 18). Kerry Packer's war. *Adelaide Now*.

Proszenko, A. (2009, November 22). Marvellous that, Richie gets better with beige. *The Sydney Morning Herald*.

—— (2011, July 3). Piggins still the people's voice. *Sydney Morning Herald*.

Sexton, J. (2013, May 5). The friends and foes of John Singleton. *The Sunday Telegraph*.

Shiel, P. (2005, December 28). A brief interlude with Kerry Packer. *The Sydney Morning Herald*.

Stone, G. (2005, December 31). In the line of fire. *The Sydney Morning Herald*.

Swanton, E. W. (1977, August). And the devil take Kerry Packer. *The Cricketer*.

Teutsch, D. (2004, April 18). The one woman in the world Kerry can't say no to. *The Sun-Herald*.

The Australian (2000, September 1).

The Bulletin Special Tribute Edition, (2006, January 4). *The Bulletin*.

Thomas, R. (2011, March 25). Packer taught Kiwi trainer a lesson. *The Daily Telegraph*.

Tycoon's gaming losses may give MGM a boost. (2000, September 6). *The Las Angeles Times*.

Wheatcroft, G. (1977, June 11). Notebook. *The Spectator*.

Woodridge, I. (1977). The London *Daily Mail*.

ACKNOWLEDGEMENTS

This book would not have been possible without the support and guidance of a small cast of people. Special thanks go to Kevin Bartlett, Dr Ian Bailey, Greg Chappell, Patrick Cook, Andrew Cowell, Graham Lawrence, Garry Linnell, Trevor Sykes and Sister Anthea Groves, for their generosity and openness. Same goes for those who asked to remain anonymous. I acknowledge, with gratitude, the authors and journalists who've gone before, in documenting the extraordinary life of Kerry Packer—for better and for worse. And finally, thanks to Mr Packer, whose Australian Consolidated Press put much of the food (and most of the magazines) on my table for almost 30 years.